CENTERBROOK

Reinventing American Architecture

Michael J. Crosbie

AIA Press

ROCKPORT PUBLISHERS

ROCKPORT, MASSACHUSETTS

DISTRIBUTED BY AIA PRESS

WASHINGTON, D.C.

First published in the United States of America by:
Rockport Publishers, Inc.
146 Granite Street
Rockport, Massachusetts 01966
Telephone: (508) 546-9590
Fax: (508) 546-7141
Telex: 5106019284 ROCKORT PUB

Distributed to the book trade and art trade in the U.S. by:
AIA Press
1735 New York Avenue NW
Washington, DC 20006
(800) 365-2724

Other Distribution by:
Rockport Publishers, Inc.
Rockport, Massachusetts 01966

ISBN 1-55835-092-6

10 9 8 7 6 5 4 3 2 1

Book Design Concept: *Group* C Inc / New Haven
Cover Design and Book Layout: Karen Gourley Lehman
Editor: Rosalie Grattaroti
Production Manager: Barbara States
Type Service Bureau: FinalCopy, Newburyport, MA

Printed in Hong Kong

Contents

Acknowledgments

Many people contributed to this book's fruition. I would like to thank James Watson and Charles Moore for their written contributions; the Centerbrook partners, principal, associates, and staff for giving freely their time and thoughts; Centerbrook clients who permitted publication of the projects; the numerous photographers who allowed use of their work; Margaret Wazuka, Chris Buckridge, and Mary Kimes for their myriad contributions with drawings and photos; Allen Freeman and Lynn Nesmith for their valuable comments and suggestions on the text; and the people at Group C, AIA Press, and Rockport Publishers.

Dedication

For Sharon, Sean, and Christopher

Foreword

In writing about Centerbrook Architects, I think first of its origins with Charles Moore, second of the many architectural victories wrought during the approaching two-decade-long span that it has served as the architect for the Cold Spring Harbor Laboratory, and third of the pleasures gained by my wife, Liz, and me in working with William Grover, the Centerbrook partner whose understated manners so belie his major talents as a designer.

In 1973 we were not looking for a clever architect to thoroughly renovate a totally rundown Airslie, the Laboratory Director's house, into which we were to move a year later. Built in 1806 for a gentleman farmer, it had been enlarged in the 1850s, and soon became a satellite house for a large estate. It already looked right in its colonial white and fitted well into the New England feeling of the shoreline on the long islet that Cold Spring Harbor makes along the North Shore of Long Island. That summer, like many before, scientists from the world of DNA-dominated research came together at Cold Spring Harbor to talk about experiments and picnic on the Airslie lawns. Ideas, not money, dominated a Cold Spring Harbor mood uncomplicated by fancy clothes or automobiles. We thus sought out a New York architect to preserve the past and to please not only our scientists but also the neighborhood community, which saw formal clothes as a necessity for Manhattan but out of place for weekends of sailing, tennis, golf, and gardening. His schematic design, however, was way off the mark for, unknown to us, he was used to working with clients who were not adverse to proclaiming their financial success through elegant Georgian features. Airslie so preserved would have given the wrong message—a misguided attempt to look backwards when the essence of science is future oriented.

We thus did a quick about face and sought out an innovative as opposed to imitative architect. Luckily, I learned that Charles Moore was the architect for a low-income housing project being built nearby. His name would have meant nothing to me except for the fact that the previous summer Liz and I had driven north along the coast above San Francisco and by total accident spent a night at the Sea Ranch Lodge. The following morning we were given a tour with the hope that we might buy a plot of land and have a home designed by one of the Moore Turnbull Lyndon Whitaker partners. On the tour we saw the now celebrated condominium building as well as many other homes that equally well excited us.

We had no idea whether this already famous man would want to associate with a farmhouse renovation guaranteed not to offend our neighbors. But he was available and shortly thereafter he and Bill Grover paid us a visit. Then we were quickly charmed by the thought that Moore might make over Airslie in the style of Sir John Soane, somehow transforming a farmhouse into a manor house. Several weeks later, on a visit to Harvard, he produced a product on a napkin and soon with Bill Grover's assistance, a real set of plans were on hand to show to my trustees. Initially I feared that opening up the center hallway to the ceiling would be judged too radical, but a new center staircase held up by very Charles Moore stage-set columns was soon accepted. When we finally moved in a year later, I was initially embarrassed by the riches of the resultant architectural triumph, elegantly presented in a green, cream, and yellow pallet.

Even more innovative was Bill Grover's scheme in 1975 for renovating our 1893 Jones Lab for experiments on nerve cells. The wainscoted shell of this almost Newport Casino building has a cathedral-like elegance revealed for the first time in its full glory by making the rooms for recording electrical impulses from nerve cells free standing units as opposed to encompassing the outer walls. Through this trick, each of the electrophysiological modules acquired separate concrete foundations, so giving to the scientists vibration free platforms on which to manipulate micropipettes into the tiny nerve cells. An ultra, almost French (Woody Allen?) high-tech feeling came from enclosing the inner rooms in aluminum sheathing. Following this major triumph in adaptive reuse, I was hooked on the consequences of good architecture.

Equal imagination went into the design of a sewage treatment plant which in our then impoverished condition had to be placed in an all too central location. Here Grover and his partner Bob Harper masked its rectangular concrete shell not only by placing much of it in a hill and topping it with a brick terrace, but by attaching a wood shingle Victorian gazebo on its waterfront side. By being so decorative a sewage plant, its function is seldom noticed, and the postcard that shows the gazebo may very well be the only one made of a modern sewage plant.

The Laboratory from across Cold Spring Harbor displays many Centerbrook creations.
Photo: Timothy Hursley

Always we have wanted to maintain our continuity with the past so that visitors returning after several years' absence still feel that the essence of our existence remains the same. For example, when in 1982 we needed to place, on the site of a falling down barn, a new building for the holding of mice and rabbits, Centerbrook designed a more modern barn with solar panels. So an undistinguished barn of wood became replaced by a second wooden edifice of greater visual distinction. Equally important has been Centerbrook's ability to actually improve the looks of existing buildings as we increased their sizes through additions. Key to our initially accepting the striking modern addition to the 1950s concrete Demerec Lab was the bold decision in 1982 to clothe it in racing green metal sheathing, giving the feeling of a green hedge planted to hide the building behind it.

After a decade necessarily preoccupied by renovations and additions, we at last had the funds in 1983 to let Centerbrook design a 360-seat auditorium to be sited virtually at the entrance to the Laboratory, just beyond and catty-corner to our marvelous, Victorian, multi-colored Davenport House. Grace Auditorium was to be our first building that proclaimed for us a university-like role. Bill Grover and Jim Childress's answer was an almost Richardsonian brick affair that might have served as a train station had it been built in the 1880s. At the same time, its massive unsymmetrical dormers and almost elephantine central columns proclaim a romantic building of today. Interestingly, this was the first auditorium ever designed by Centerbrook and not surprisingly is as unsymmetrical on the inside as outside. Again they managed to profoundly change our appearance in ways that made us even more of what we have always been.

Front hall of the newly
renovated Airslie House.
Photo: Norman McGrath

An even bigger opportunity for success or failure came with the Laboratory's decision to create essentially a second campus on the hillside above the main Lab. Here was the space needed for a major new complex containing a new laboratory for Neurobiology and a new residence hall needed to replace an un-inspired, motel-like one story wooden building from the 1950s. Initially we thought Adirondack style wooden buildings were needed to blend unnoticed into the forest scene above us, and Centerbrook gave us such a scheme. But the visual success of Grace Auditorium later on gave us the courage to ask whether we should not only act like a university but look like one. I remember telling Bill Grover that the mood of the new campus should be postmodern, collegiate Gothic encompassing a courtyard as well as a diminutive rendition of a Philip Johnson-like skyscraper bearing a large bell. Charles Moore emerged for two days of talking, but it was Grover and Childress who gave us the basic design plan—all in less than six weeks to met an early November 1987 deadline created by the visit of a potential donor. The courtyard sited bell tower was there, adjacent to the main laboratory, but most certainly not Gothic nor of any style gone before. With more bricks at the top than on the bottom, looking initially almost like a folly but in fact containing the smokestacks, Hazen Tower dominates our new Cathedral of Learning.

Already we have several more Centerbrook design projects within our sights and so stand apart from most academic institutions which never seem to want a return visit from their latest architect, no matter how highly esteemed. In part the reason is that Centerbrook's partners, in particular Bill Grover, act like true gentlemen and treat their clients with great respect. If we do not like some aspect of a plan, Bill is always willing to consider changes and actually will make them! At no time have they used their positions as experts to imply that we don't know what we want. Of course, if on our side we were architectural ignoramuses this approach could quickly have led to repeated disasters. But in Jack Richards, its director of the Building and Grounds Department, the Cold Spring Harbor Laboratory possesses a high quality contractor who knows what an architectural plan actually specifies.

Equally important, first Liz and then I early on developed real interests in architecture—both of the past and present. Architectural magazines dominate our house as much as *Nature* and *Science*. And as the effective manager of a very large estate, I look forward to reading *Country Life* even more than I do the weekly *Economist*. Of course, if the latest received Centerbrook design was more of the same or indistinguishable from the common variety postmodern designs of suburbia, we would become bored and concentrate our thoughts on Centerbrook's minor errors in projects past. Hopefully, this will never occur with their always presenting solutions that we have never seen before. This will not be an easy task and their success can never be foreordained. In that sense, good architecture is much like science at its best—great fun, but sometimes scary.

James D. Watson
Cold Spring Harbor, New York

*I*NTRODUCTION

Michael J. Crosbie

Essex, Connecticut, with a population of under 5,000, has managed to survive into the late 20th century with much of its early American character intact. Stately 18th and 19th century houses that line its Main Street, along with one of America's oldest inns, the Griswold, attract day-trippers from far and wide, who totter off tourist buses to soak up a bit of authentic, vanishing New England. All of this might make Essex an unlikely place to find one of the country's leading design firms, but the small-town locale bespeaks much of what Centerbrook Architects, and its work, is all about.

Centerbrook occupies a carefully tended, small congeries of rambling industrial buildings that are emblematic of the firm's architecture: a respect but not veneration of buildings that have come before and attention to architecture's habitation in the landscape. The firm actually started in New Haven, Connecticut, as a transplantation of Charles Moore's Berkeley, California, architectural partnership, Moore Lyndon Turnbull Whitaker. In 1965 Moore headed east from Berkeley to assume the chair of Yale University's department of architecture.

After several years of practice and one too many burglaries of Moore's house and studio on New Haven's Elm Street, his associate and former student, William Grover, discovered an abandoned auger bit factory, constructed in 1874, on the banks of the Falls River in the village of Centerbrook, part of the town of Essex, 35 miles east of New Haven. Fleeing the crime, traffic, and grime of the city, Moore's firm purchased the factory in 1970 and renovated it into studios. A Victorian cottage just west of the factory became Moore's home (it is now the site for office ping-pong tournaments). In 1975 Moore returned to California to head yet another school and start yet another firm, and Charles Moore Associates became Moore Grover Harper.

Centerbrook's staff, by the dam.

More than twenty years later, Centerbrook Architects (which changed its name from Moore Grover Harper in 1984) enjoys its privileged location, continuing to practice in the factory by the river. A major flood that in 1982 swept away a hodge-podge of shacks behind the factory presented an opportunity to expand the office with several new buildings that reflect the character of the old mill. A water turbine generator in the bowels of the factory was replaced and now supplies additional electric power. The landscape, which includes a waterfall just beyond the office, is manicured. At dawn, at sunset, or on a crisp autumn day, with golden light reflecting off the river, Centerbrook's home borders on the idyllic. It is a world in miniature that demonstrates, not unlike enclaves such as Taliesin and Cranbrook, the architectural values and attention to the creation of place shared by the people who work there.

While the exterior of Centerbrook's home for the most part "keeps the faith" of small-town New England—its modifications and refinements affirming the local context—the interior communicates the energy, creativity, and fun present in Centerbrook's architecture. Over the front door hangs a moose head, a gift to

Charles Moore from a client, who claimed it to be the largest moose ever shot in Alaska by a woman prior to 1912. A waterfall of steps transports you to reception, an area studded with almost every conceivable architectural prize, from AIA National Honor Awards to recognition from the Pope himself for the design of a church.

Just beyond the reception area is the main drafting room, where, a century before, leather belts and flywheels propelled bit-making machinery. Today, there is just the low hum of CAD machines and plotters. The drafting room is one large space, its open roof trusses fitted out with zig-zags of fluorescent lights. The oak plank floors are worn and creaky, the exposed brick walls patched and patinated. Architectural models occupy nearly every horizontal surface that isn't being used for

TOP: Centerbrook's offices overlook the Falls River.
Photo: Timothy Hursley

ABOVE: Near the office entrance, architectural accolades and a stuffed moose.
Photo: Timothy Hursley

drawing—some are for presentation and others are for design study. There is a layer of bricolage throughout the office: mirrored column capitals from the Venice Biennale; sheet metal brackets salvaged from demolished buildings in New York City and Columbus, Ohio; a doll house made of weathered linoleum and asphalt shingles; a model ship; a sample board of neon lights; Bill Grover's trumpet. The environment is warm, relaxed, open, colorful, unpretentious, funky.

"The quality of this place that attracted me the first time I walked through the door was that it reminded me of my studio at architecture school," comments Mahdad Saniee, one of Centerbrook's dozen associates. "If it gets a little messy, no one cares." Unlike many firms whose offices attempt to awe with over-wrought design, Centerbrook communicates an architectural sensibility with calculated casualness. "Most architects think that they're going to impress clients with a fabulous bolt detail," says Mark Simon. "We show them a stuffed moose instead. They notice the colors, the comfort, and the strange things on the walls." Simon is one of five Centerbrook partners. The others are Bill Grover, Bob Harper, Jeff Riley, and Chad Floyd.

"Most clients love coming out here because it feels like they're on vacation," says Grover, and the locale does offer palpable advantages over the press and hustle of architect enclaves such as New York, Chicago, and Los Angeles where firms are pursuing work as significant as Centerbrook's. Many of the 50-person staff live nearby; some bicycle or walk to work. There's parking space at the front door, a good restaurant across the street, less crime, better schools—the tangible benefits of small-town life. And with fax machines, express delivery, computers, airports, and reliable consultants close at hand, there are no drawbacks to practicing architecture in Essex. Except one—luring bright, new talent fresh from architecture school. In a town where the only traffic light shuts off at 9 PM, it's sometimes difficult to attract young interns seeking after-hours diversions. "If you're single, the social life can be terrible," Simon admits, "but many are willing to commute from New Haven."

Whether the choice of where to practice reflects what to practice, or the practice reflects its locale, the building traditions and values of the small New England town are bound up in Centerbrook's architectural creations. "This setting is what we're about," offers Floyd, "constantly refining, making it better, but not being too precious about it, fitting in with the old village. It becomes part of the framework that informs our view of architecture. It sensitizes us to New England and its traditions, but it also alerts us to the context and values that exist in the various places around the country where we design buildings. Compared to Europe, America's cities and communities have a relatively weak context. Successive generations which have not shared basic attitudes about design have left little continuity. In our design work we attempt to find places where we can seam together pieces of the environment that have been ripped. It may be only a memory of what was there, or ought to be there, or a wish. It's more than just paying attention to buildings immediately adjacent to your project. It's the community's history, its traditions, its memories." Riley describes a value shared in the work of all the partners as a search for genuineness: "The notion that architecture should be genuine, meaningful, honest, and lasting. It should have a sense of permanence." There is an emphasis on architecture's experiential qualities, a general disdain for dry formalism, and integration of buildings into the landscape. This last quality the partners attribute to their long and fruitful collaboration with landscape architect Lester Collins.

The main drafting room in the renovated 1870s factory building.
Photo: Timothy Hursley

In her insightful study of the profession, *Architecture: The Story of Practice*, Dana Cuff concludes that "the excellent architectural office...appears to have strong leadership, a loose organizational structure, a respect for creative genius, a clear set of values, informal, face-to-face communication, and a high standard of quality.... The architect whose name is on the door is actively involved throughout the project, acting as head designer and manager without substituting an impenetrable layer of management between the head and those who get the work done."

Cuff's description, multiplied by five, could be Centerbrook. The office is essentially five practices under one roof. Unlike traditional American architecture firms, there are no "design" partners, "business" partners, "marketing" partners, or

Roger Williams (left) and
Mark Simon ponder a design.
Photo: Margaret Wazuka

"production" partners. Each partner is responsible for bringing in his own commissions, negotiating the contracts, designing the projects, meeting with clients and consultants, overseeing the construction documents, and administrating construction. The associates work directly with the partners in varying degrees of collaboration; their roles involve everything from sharing design decisions to attending to a project's minutiae.

Likewise, the architectural staff is not segregated into "design" departments and "production" departments. Everyone does a bit of everything. This organization is apparent in the physical setting of the office. Throughout the several buildings that Centerbrook occupies, partners, associates, and architectural staff all sit in the same drafting room and at the same sized desks. There are no partitions or private offices. Business cards bear no titles. Even the dress code is egalitarian: neck ties are the exception; flannel shirts, jeans, and loafers are common attire—although partners (save for Grover) do tend to dress up.

The casualness, however, should not be interpreted as inattentiveness. The high quality of the design work and its execution is due to a pervasive ethic of persistence to maintain the office standard. The partners' involvement in every aspect of a project—from the basic design concept to the selection of finish screws—grows from a desire for maximum control over (and responsibility for) the end product.

This extent of the partners' governance over the projects, uncommon in most firms of this size, is attributed by Chad Floyd to the nature of the staff. "We have a strong set of associates, very capable people, who manage the day-to-day details of a job so that the partners are free to design. In most other firms the partners are the ones who manage and the junior people are the designers. Although there's collaboration here on design and management, the talents of the staff allow the partners the freedom to shepherd the design all the way through to the building's completion."

The arrangement does have a disadvantage: With such personal attention, there's a limit to the number of projects one partner can handle. And that limit regulates the size of the firm, which has remained at about 50 people for the past few years. "We got up to about 60 people once, and it was not fun," Grover recalls. "If you're not having fun, it's usually the result of having too many things to do, and not doing them well enough."

The partners share a belief in the importance of relating architecture to its physical and social context. They describe this approach as "situationist" design: that every piece of architecture has a duty to respond to the specific demands of the client, the site, the people who will use the building, the community at large, and the budget. But it must also incorporate the intangible: a spirit of the time, a client's fantasy, a passage from a

The Miller House's agrarian forms.
Photo: Jeff Goldberg/Esto

book, the memory of a another place, poetry.

Being a good listener and flexible in the design's development are cornerstones in this approach. The logistics of listening well when dealing with a single individual, such as a house client, are relatively simple. In the design of public buildings or private institutions, however, Centerbrook often relies on a "design workshop" to gather as many ideas as possible. At the outset of the design of a university student center, for example, students, teachers, administrative staff, trustees, and maintenance staff will be brought together for a five or six-day session at the proposed project site. The participants walk the site with the architects, take photographs, discuss the design possibilities. Back in the workshop, large rolls of paper cover the floor, everyone is given color felt markers, Scotch tape, construction paper, and other graphic tools, and each is asked to draw his or her ideal student center, indicating what its spaces might be like, what adjacencies it might have to other campus buildings, and what kind of materials might be used. "The design workshop is like a town meeting," says principal Jim Childress, "where everyone is involved in the design process, but according to a clear decision-making framework that we establish." Leonard J. Wyeth, an associate, adds that the workshop "demystifies the art of architecture. When you involve the clients intimately, you strip away the mystique of design."

The most extensive use of the design workshop has been in Centerbrook's work in Dayton, Ohio; Springfield, Massachusetts; Watkins Glen, New York; and Roanoke, Virginia; where the process was used to develop urban design strategies. In those cities the intimate workshops were coupled with design sessions broadcast on local commercial and public prime time television, which allowed tens of thousands of viewers to have a say in the design of their communities.

Flexibility is evident in the architect's willingness to change the design in response to client wishes—another quality inherited from Moore. "In reading *The Fountainhead*, Charles said that he always identified more with Peter Keating than with Howard Roark," muses Bill Grover. "Whenever a client was unhappy with something, Keating was ready to accommodate him. Roark would rather blow the building up than change it. Chuck's theory is that there are at least a million different answers to a design problem. The true genius is the one who can satisfy everybody and get a great building out of it, rather than the architect who comes up with one design and tells the client its the only answer to all his problems. Accommodation is a way of designing that has stuck with us."

Of course, accommodation must be tempered with the architect's knowledge about what will and won't work.

Giving clients everything they want, or changing the design at the drop of a hat, can be reckless and, on the part of the architect, irresponsible. "I've had instances where clients said, after the building was completed, that they wished I had tried harder to talk them out of something that they were set on," admits Grover. Jeff Riley believes that the designer has an obligation to defend an idea, "until you're convinced, beyond a doubt, that the client understands exactly what you've proposed. If you've fully explained the idea through models and drawings, and the client has a complete understanding of the design and still doesn't like it, then it's time to change it and move on."

Like members of a family, Centerbrook's partners share a bedrock of architectural value. But each has his own design personality and sensibilities. Grover is influenced by old factory buildings, industrial architecture, barns, hand tools, objects of utilitarian simplicity. "The gable-roof box, to me, is the essence of a building," he notes, albeit a New England building. "I like hardware stores, parts out of catalogs that already exist that you can combine in new ways—making something elegant out of something cheap. Ordinary things can be wonderful, and frugal. Architecture ought to be amusing too." Grover's design for the Miller House in the Berkshire Mountains of Massachusetts seems to capture many of these qualities. Composed of simple, agrarian shapes and colors, the house dovetails with its rural location. The Baldwin House in Essex shares many of the Miller House's attributes in its large, simple shapes, use of materials, and open interior. Yet the two buildings are quite different—shaped by their clients and sites.

Williams College Museum of Art's historicist interior.
Photo: Steve Rosenthal

Harper possesses an academician's approach to design and a thorough understanding of structure and construction—a combination not found in many practitioners. In the Rudolph House in Williamstown, Massachusetts, Harper uses a classical arrangement of spaces straight from Palladio, adapting them to the lot's vigorous contours. In fact, the stasis of the classical plan is a deft foil for the sloped site, each pointing up the extreme of the other. The Williams College Museum of Art, also in Williamstown, marries an early 19th century building with an angled new addition that reiterates the geometry of the former to make the whole intelligible. "In plan, when you see this addition sitting at a strange angle to the original, you wonder what's it all about," says Harper of the design. "But experiencing the building as it sits on its sloping site, you understand where the angle came from." Harper's restrained exteriors often wrap spatial surprises inside.

Of the five partners, Simon is perhaps the best read architecturally, and the most cerebral. Books surround his desk, and he soaks up design ideas like a sponge, transforming them and combining them with a twist. His floor plans can be quite similar in their elemental parti, but result in radically different buildings in response to client and place. A comparison of the Ross-Lacy House and the

TOP: The Ross-Lacy House interprets the tradition of Greek Revival.
Photo: Timothy Hursley

ABOVE: Curved sea forms are alluded to in the Reid House II.
Photo: Timothy Hursley

Marsh Estate partis, for example, reveals parallels in plan, but divaricated buildings in three dimensions. Simon's fascination with carving geometric shapes out of solid blocks of poché, again in plan, is a re-occurring theme. A collage of recollected images that Simon discovers with clients and then transforms are layered with strong figural spaces, making each building distinctive. "The result shouldn't appear as though it happened by accident," explains Simon. "The elements should belong together—should seem inevitable that they were put together in that way. What's especially exciting is that I don't think that requires a hermetic style, old or new. The development of a personal, recognizable character—a signature—is not necessary. I look to Picasso and Eero Saarinen to remind me that it's possible to be good and still change your imagery, to not repeat yourself over and over again."

Riley's approach to design is intuitive. Of the five he draws the best, and his buildings are often fanciful and decorative. Riley's designs are strongest in all three dimensions. He builds layer upon layer of space, and then punches holes through the layers to reveal one pocket of space to another. This makes for some surprising spatial juxtapositions: views from the bedrooms down into the living room of the Reid House in Ohio, for example, or his own house in Guilford, Connecticut. Riley's signature swirls and curls, which are meant to prompt associations with life forms and anatomical shapes, are used to best effect in moderation, such as the column capitals in his own kitchen, or when they forge connections with a project's context, such as with sea-life in the Reid House on Cape Cod. Another common theme is the building as a village, where a family for forms are arranged along a path, like buildings along a street. The Elliott House in Ligonier, Pennsylvania, is one of the best examples of this approach—a veritable village within a house.

In his work in Roanoke, Virginia, Floyd reveals his talents as an architect of orchestration. His invention of the televised design workshop is a brilliant architectural foray into mass-media. Floyd has translated architecture's language into a format intelligible within the confines of a TV tube, which is, perhaps, where every bit of our culture is ultimately headed. He made the tube interactive with the viewer, and by extension made architectural design the purview of the couch potato. Before studying architecture Floyd was involved in theatre, and his buildings are often conceived with a director's eye——how one will approach the building, cross the threshold, move through space, how views will be framed. This is particularly evident in projects such as the Hood Museum of Art at Dartmouth College, where one's first view of the building is as if through a proscenium arch. At a much smaller scale, Floyd's design for Samuel's clothing store in Roanoke is essentially a stage set that uses lighting and movable props to set the mood.

Centerbrook departs from the Moore tradition of design collaboration among partners. At MLTW, for example, all four partners were involved with the design of each project. This is still the case for Moore Ruble Yudell Architects in Santa Monica, California. In the early years at Centerbrook, the partners did collaborate (particularly when there were more partners than projects). The structure of separate practices evolved slowly, and it was a conscious decision that no partner would have design jurisdiction over another. However, "design in the open" and not in private offices leads to casual critiques of the work among the partners.

Collaboration does occur between partners and associates, although there is an undertow of frustration among the associates as to the degree of design freedom allowed. "Some partners are reluctant to pass the pencil around," comments one associate, "and if the pencil is passed, are unwilling to recognize the contributions of others." The reason for this may be that the partners themselves are still emerging from the shadow of Charles Moore, and on occasion their work is erroneously identified as his. Moore's relation with Centerbrook today is as a design consultant, who may drop in twice a year to noodle around on a project, or join forces with a partner to fetch a commission, or participate in a design workshop. Another associate sees it this way: "To the partners' credit, they have a reluctance to let someone cut loose and do whatever they want. There's a desire to keep the image of the firm and the work at the top of the line, all the way through."

As befits its architecture, Centerbrook does not engage in polemics. There is commitment to good design, without over-wrought theory. There is appreciation for materials and their joining, without academic mysticism. There is sensitivity to the past, without sentimentality. There is willingness to listen, without abdication of design responsibility. Perhaps Bill Grover's gentle dictum, the closest thing to a Centerbrook manifesto, sums it up best: "We're going to make good architecture, we're going to have fun making it, and we're going to make enough money to keep going. In that order."

The Hood Museum of Art is framed by a proscenium arch.
Photo: Timothy Hursley

Riley House

In 1976 Jeff Riley built a small, 1,300-square-foot solar heated house for his family of three. The house was tall, with a long gable roof, dormers, central chimney, and overall bilateral symmetry offset by asymmetrical parts. It made allusions to colonial houses and cottages indigenous to its New England context, but was conceived as vernacular with contemporary translation. The first floor, entered through a greenhouse, contained a large open kitchen/dining/living space, with three bedrooms on the second and third floors, which step back with smaller dormers.

By 1986, the family had grown to five, and was pushing the spatial envelope of the first-floor all-purpose room. A new, symmetrical wing added a formal, entertainment retreat to a previously informal, family house. A new master bedroom cantilevers over the living room. The family opted for more comforts in the new living spaces: baseboard heating under the window seats, a fireplace for atmosphere, and elegant windows facing everywhere but south. The addition also provides places of repose, such as a sitting room corner nestled in the master bedroom.

A desire for more languorous living also brought on the need for methodical storage in the form of a pantry creating the bridge between the old kitchen and the new dining room. Additional counter space allows more cooks to get involved in the preparations, yet stay out of each other's way. The new formal entry also provides a contrary sort of formality—no traditional hallway divides living and dining rooms, and guests enter the house asymmetrically, off axis, facing the symmetrical living room fireplace, their ultimate destination.

ABOVE: Kitchen interior has a soaring two-story space.
Photo: Norman McGrath

LEFT AND OPPOSITE:
Original house had a tight, sculptural form.
Photo: Norman McGrath

LEFT: Later addition to right of original house gives it a manor bearing.
Photo: Peter Mauss/Esto

BELOW: Addition's living room offers secluded nooks for conversation.
Photo: Norman McGrath

OPPOSITE TOP: New front entry leads to a sunny foyer.
Photo: Norman McGrath

OPPOSITE BOTTOM: Dining is on axis with fireplace in new living room.
Photo: Norman McGrath

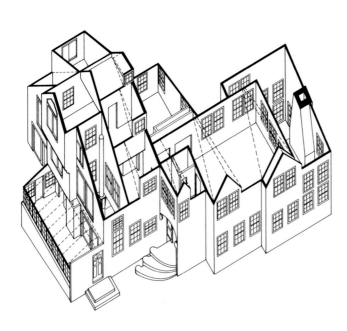

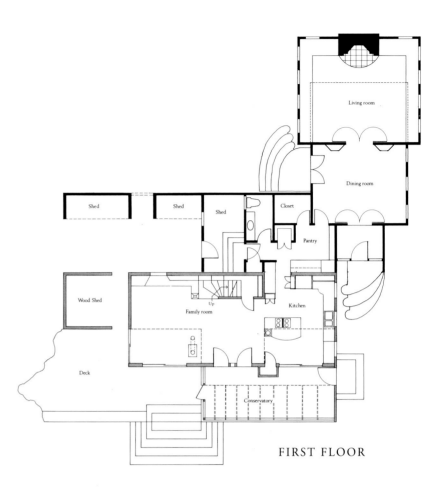

FIRST FLOOR

$\mathcal{J}$ones Laboratory

The renovation of the Jones laboratory dramatically combines the old and the new. The exterior of the century-old structure (Cold Spring Harbor Laboratory's first building) was immaculately restored, and inside the existing ceiling and walls of yellow pine were patched, cleaned, and varnished.

The interior, however, presented a challenge in adapting a quaint old lab for state-of-the art electrophysiology research. This dictated that each lab area be isolated from other lab spaces and the building itself to avoid acoustical, electrical, or vibration disturbance of the highly sensitive instruments and experiment procedures.

The solution was to isolate each lab on its own foundation and shield it electrically from its neighbors by a grounded aluminum skin. Precise temperatures are maintained in the labs, while greater variations in temperature can be tolerated in the spaces between the aluminum pods. These "between" spaces widen at an old stone fireplace at the center of one of the lab's two long walls. Here are comfortable chairs and an atmosphere congenial to relaxation and discussion, because learning and research happen not only in the lab spaces, but also in the places where scientists meet and talk with each other informally.

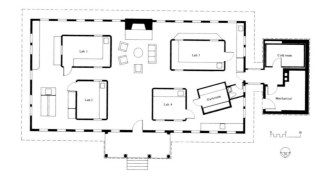

ABOVE: Lounge areas are close to pods and grouped around fireplace.
Photo: Norman McGrath

RIGHT: Aluminum clad lab pods contrast with warmth of wood.
Photo: Norman McGrath

OPPOSITE ABOVE: Original 19th century interior of laboratory.

OPPOSITE INSET: Exterior is preserved with late 19th century character.
Photo: Susan Lauter

$\mathcal{W}$aste Water Treatment Plant

Cold Spring Harbor Laboratory
Cold Spring Harbor, New York

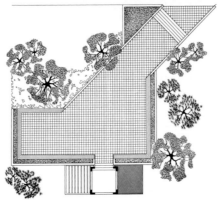

TERRACE LEVEL

The various waste products generated by a biological laboratory are complex and need special treatment before they can be returned to the ground water system. As the lab grew, its sand-filter water treatment system became inadequate and a new system would have to occupy the same site because all the waste pipes from the various lab buildings terminated there. This location happened to be one of the most beautiful spots on the laboratory grounds for viewing Cold Spring Harbor. A large building was required to house the water treatment equipment, and there was concern that it would block views to the harbor, as well as be unsightly in its own right.

The solution was to bury the equipment building deep into the natural hillside, staying above the high water line, and make it a visual asset rather than a liability. The building is constructed of reinforced concrete, its concrete plank roof covered with a brick terrace. The existing hillside was regraded around and on top of the building, and extensive planting and landscaping was done. The building's east side, which faces the harbor, sports a wood-shingled gazebo topped by a copper finial, made by Bill Grover, modeled after the adenovirus molecule, used in cancer research at Cold Spring Harbor Laboratory. It is hoped that when visitors visit the lab, they will be impressed by the beauty of the natural surroundings and the gazebo, and unaware that a waste treatment plant exists beneath it.

OPPOSITE: Picturesque gazebo sits atop the treatment plant.
Photo: Ross Meurer

LEFT: Finial atop gazebo is modeled after adenovirus molecule.
Photo: Susan Lauter

BELOW: Gazebo offers quiet setting for harbor views.
Photo: Nick Wheeler

*D*elbruck-Page Laboratory

The Delbruck-Page Laboratory is actually a series of additions to a lab constructed in 1926. The first addition connects to the south of the original shingle-clad colonial style building via a dark glass corridor, which, from a distance, blends into the background. The disappearing connector allows the gabled profiles of the lab to be read clearly and reinforces the "village" look of the harbor. Like the original building, the first addition is oriented with its long axis perpendicular to the harbor.

A second addition five years later added another gable-roofed lab to the north of the 1926 building, connected likewise with a glassy corridor. Most of the more recent addition's lab spaces are located below the main floor, but due to the sloping site there are views of the harbor from all work stations. The building contains laboratories, equipment rooms, and offices for scientists.

Each of the two additions is somewhat different in shape, fenestration, trim, and color, reflecting the diversity that one might expect from buildings constructed at different times for different reasons.

ABOVE LEFT: Page addition uses many details found in region's colonial architecture.
Photo: Susan Lauter

OPPOSITE: Laboratory's three gabled forms as they face the harbor.
Photo: Margot Bennett

MAIN FLOOR

*D*emerec Laboratory Addition

ABOVE: Green addition nudges next to 1950s concrete bunker.
Photo: Margot Bennett

OPPOSITE: Viewed from south, addition appears as a large shrub.
Photo: Andrew Garn, reproduced with permission of Cold Spring Harbor Laboratory Press

In the early years of recombinant DNA experiments, Cold Spring Harbor arranged with Exxon Corporation to expand the former's existing Demerec Laboratory, which was built in 1953. The Exxon collaboration would provide approximately 5,000 square feet of laboratory and equipment spaces to be used for teaching Exxon scientists the basic principles of recombinant DNA technology.

The original Demerec lab is hardly a building sympathetic to the older architecture of Cold Spring Harbor. A chilly, raw, concrete box, it was designed and built at the height of the Cold War, when institutional buildings took on the appearance of concrete bunkers and bomb shelters.

Frank Lloyd Wright once counseled a young apprentice that a physician can bury his mistakes, but the best an architect can do is plant vines. The design of the new addition was conceived in the spirit of Wright's advice. "Building as foundation planting" was the guiding concept for the Demerec addition, which is planted on the south side of the original lab, appearing as a large green shrub to effectively hide the concrete bunker. The exterior material, a sandwich panel of aluminum and polyethylene, was chosen for its dark green color and for the fact that it can be bent into curved shapes. The rounded top edge of the addition is a parapet which hides a large collection of mechanical equipment. Two green cylindrical tubes provide exhaust for numerous fume hoods, an emergency generator, and a host of utilities.

Controversial at first, Demerec's addition now plays its horticultural role quietly, receiving very little notice from passersby.

*G*race Auditorium

Grace Auditorium is the home of the annual Cold Spring Harbor Symposium, along with several large meetings and courses held during the year. The 20,000-square-foot building contains, on the ground floor, a 360-seat lecture hall with audiovisual capabilities, a light filled lobby, and offices for public affairs. On the lower level are other offices, a computer center, and the Biotechnology Resource Center.

The building is framed in steel, enclosed with concrete block, and veneered in alternating courses of terra-cotta color and dark brown brick. The entry portico features a roof which is an extension of the shallow hipped roof of the building itself, and is sheathed with Vermont slate. Four dormer windows pierce the main roof in a highly asymmetrical fashion.

Part of the building is built into a hillside, thus providing a year-round moderating influence on the interior environment. A covered piazza which runs nearly the entire length of the south facade helps shade that side during the summer months. Dormer windows are positioned so as to receive directly the rays of the winter sun. Solar warmth that enters the building via these windows is stored in two solid masonry interior walls.

On the interior of the auditorium are colors that allude to the out-of-doors. Pale whites, trimmed in dark green, rise to a band of midnight blue, decorated by a frieze depicting the spiralling DNA molecule.

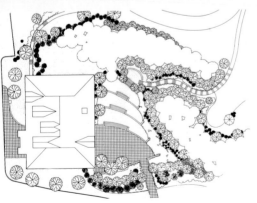

ABOVE: Auditorium is decorated with a stenciled frieze of DNA molecule.
Photo: Peter Aaron/Esto

OPPOSITE: Glowing dormers mark auditorium and provide mystery.
Photo: Peter Aaron/Esto

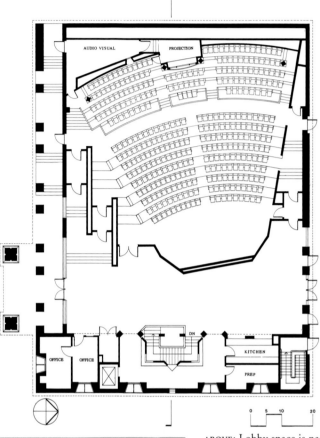

ABOVE: Lobby space is naturally illuminated with daylight from above.
Photo: Peter Aaron/Esto

LEFT: Entry to the auditorium is under large porch.
Photo: Peter Aaron/Esto

OPPOSITE: Lobby windows frame view to north side plaza.
Photo: Peter Aaron/Esto

$\mathcal{N}$euroscience Center

ABOVE: Laboratory blends
into hillside overlooking Cold
Spring Harbor.
Photo: Timothy Hursley

OPPOSITE: Laboratory and
residence hall define courtyard.
Photo: Timothy Hursley

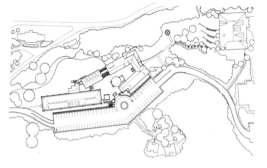

SITE PLAN

Although Cold Spring Harbor Laboratory is at the vanguard of research on cancer and molecular genetics, it still retains the aspect of a serene New England village. For the Neuroscience Center, Laboratory Director James D. Watson sought a substantial, academic type of architecture. The hillside site can be viewed from across the harbor in the context of surrounding residentially scaled buildings. This new complex, which includes housing for 60 visiting scientists, is located on the site of a motel structure which provided summer housing for the lab.

The interior character of this complex is organized around two ideas: first, that interaction among scientists is important to the generation of ideas and discovery. Second, the nature of research changes so the facilities for it must be flexible at a reasonable cost and with the least disruption of scientific work.

The exterior is also based on two ideas: first, that Cold Spring Harbor Laboratory is becoming an educational institution in a permanent year-round sense and, therefore, its new buildings should be characterized by the more substantial feeling of an academic campus. Second, this academic community is located in a beautiful and historic residential community, and its buildings should fit comfortably with their neighbors.

The Neuroscience Center is designed to be a "generic" structure which can easily accommodate the many changes that scientific institutions undergo as the direction of basic research changes over the years. The laboratory and the residence hall form an outdoor courtyard, which is the entrance to both. Across this courtyard the two buildings frame views of Cold Spring Harbor to the east. The campanile at the northwest corner contains, in addition to its bell, a stairway from the second floor of the lab, and the chimneys from the mechanical room below the courtyard.

ABOVE: Laboratory seminar room looks out onto courtyard and harbor.
Photo: Timothy Hursley

RIGHT: View from residence hall of laboratory at dusk.
Photo: Timothy Hursley

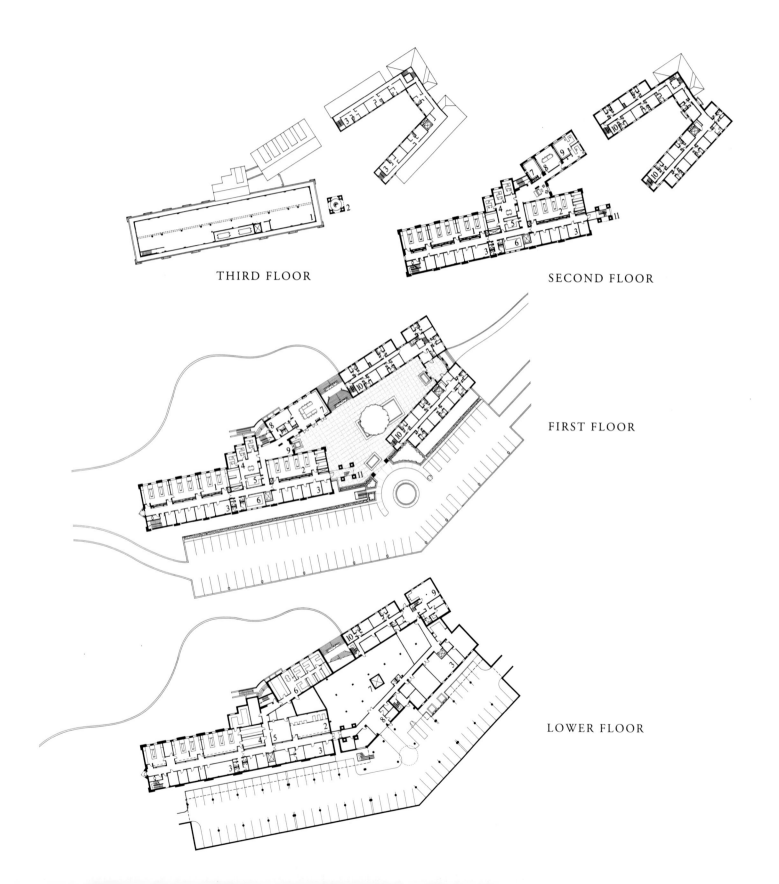

THIRD FLOOR

SECOND FLOOR

FIRST FLOOR

LOWER FLOOR

LEFT: Harbor view is gained between laboratory and residence hall.
Photo: Jeff Goldberg/Esto

BELOW LEFT: Building is a phalanx as it faces east.
Photo: Jeff Goldberg/Esto

BELOW: Tower surmounts steps from harbor side.
Photo: Jeff Goldberg/Esto

CLOCKWISE FROM TOP:
Approach to residence hall
from the south.
Photo: Timothy Hursley

Residence hall defines south
end of courtyard.
Photo: Timothy Hursley

Verde granite clad entry to
laboratory.
Photo: Timothy Hursley

$\mathcal{R}$udolph House

ABOVE: Segmented dome in living room admits natural light from above.
Photo: Joseph Standart

OPPOSITE: Illuminated north elevation provides backdrop for pool.
Photo: Joseph Standart

Classical forms in architecture set up visual expectations. When viewing Palladio's Villa Rotunda on its hilltop site, we see a familiar and stable relationship between villa and land. We infer from the roof and porticos what the villa's other elevations are like. The Villa Barbaro is built against a hillside, but because the hill rises from front to back, the house is seen in a stable relationship to its site and our visual expectations are not at first disturbed.

The site of this house is a long, sloping meadow, easily accessible only from the south by moving along the side of the hill. The best view is to the north—agreeable in a house that is primarily used in spring, summer, and fall. The clients asked for major spaces, indoor and out, to be on one level. This determined a sequential arrangement of drive, motor court, house, and pool court along the axis of movement across the site, with the meadow rising to the east and falling away to the west. The level floor of the house along the axis is in strong and apparent contrast with the sloping site.

The living room is central to the house. Double walls around and a dome over this space define the heart of the house and allow daylight from above to enliven the living room without endangering antique furniture, books, or paintings. The kitchen is found to the east and a bedroom to the west. Studies occupy the west pavilions; dining room and laundry occupy those to the east. On the lower floor, open to grade, bedrooms and baths accommodate visiting children and grandchildren.

The use of classical forms in this house exploits the tension between landscape, house, and the axial organization of the house itself. The classical forms set up expectations, but the site challenges them at once.

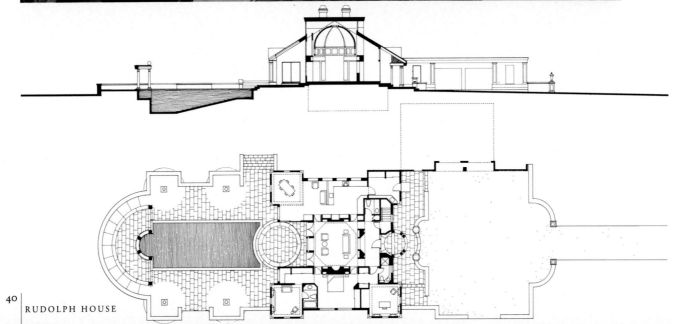

CLOCKWISE FROM TOP LEFT:
North facade overlooks pool as
site slopes east to west.
Photo: Joseph Standart

Symmetrical south facade from
driveway approach.
Photo: Joseph Standart

House as it rises against the
landscape.
Photo: Joseph Standart

OPPOSITE: At the heart of the
house is domed living room.
Photo: Joseph Standart

$\mathcal{R}$oanoke Design

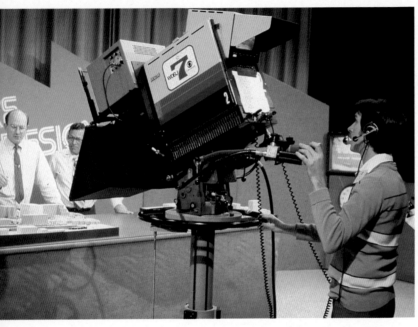

ABOVE: Television design sessions engaged the entire community.

OPPOSITE TOP: Master plan model as unveiled in last of four television shows.

OPPOSITE BOTTOM: New farmer's market is critical part of downtown's rebirth.

After several decades of decline, the city of Roanoke, Virginia, called upon Centerbrook to design a redevelopment plan that would revitalize its faltering downtown. Taking a novel approach, Centerbrook enlisted Roanoke residents as "design consultants." The architects set up shop in a storefront, laying the groundwork for developing the design, inviting people in to give their impressions of what was wrong with Roanoke and how it could be made better, discussing their ideas over drawing pads, magic markers, and coffee.

To engage Roanoke citizens at large, four public design sessions were broadcast on a local television channel. The first of the Roanoke "Design-a-Thons" introduced the redevelopment design team, outlined its objectives, and encouraged viewers to call in with their ideas. The project area was presented using a brightly colored map and graphics, which comprised 280 acres in the city's downtown business section. As various aspects of the plan were discussed, viewers called a number on the television screen to offer their ideas, which were relayed to the show's architect hosts, who discussed them on the air and drew conceptual sketches of the ideas. The end of the show presented a re-cap of the ideas collected, and the architects returned to their storefront design center to consider each one.

The next three shows built on the groundwork laid in the first. The last show presented the plan in its completed form, including 59 individual projects requiring $47.2 million in public investment and $17.2 in private investment. Within three years Roanoke citizens voted for bond issues to fund all but seven of these projects. Centerbrook has used this same approach to answer the particular needs of downtown areas in Dayton, Ohio; Springfield, Massachusetts; and Watkins Glen, New York.

$\mathcal{R}$oanoke Markethouse

The Markethouse is an interior renovation of an early-20th century, neo-Georgian building. It had fallen into relative disuse over the course of the 1960s, and '70s, and was threatened with demolition. Saved in the late-1970s by preservationists, it still was left without a viable economic function. Centerbrook's Design '79 study revitalizing Roanoke identified the building as an urban landmark with development potential. In 1985 the study resulted in the building's development into a new marketplace.

The few remaining butchers and fishmongers from those who years before had filled the City Market were moved to low-rent spaces across the street. Farmer's stalls were built within the surrounding urban square to replace the produce stand which once had occupied the perimeter of the Markethouse. With these activities arrayed around the Markethouse, the stage was set for returning the building to the color and bustle of a traditional marketplace, incorporating modern retailing.

The interior ground floor was developed into small food stalls along a central north-south axis, requiring a strong system to organize the resulting visual cacophony. This was provided by columns and overhead steel mezzanine railings punctuated by a rhythm of surface-lit, hand-painted signs. To provide cohesiveness, each retailer was asked to convey his offerings with a simple picture, sans words.

The bazaar of stalls is anchored at the center with a large octagonal eating space. All infrastructure was painted in a palette of dark, cool colors to contrast with the warm tones of the stalls. A middle-value, polychrome quarry tile covers the floor. Atmosphere is heightened by an overhead strip of neon configured at the central space into a dome in the shape of an eight-pointed star, based on the "star" symbol of Roanoke.

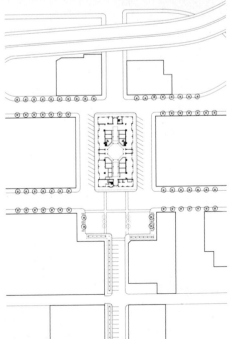

ABOVE: Heart of markethouse interior is transformed by neon light.
Photo: Norman McGrath.

LEFT: Illuminated graphic signage adds festive flair.
Photo: Norman McGrath

OPPOSITE: The markethouse becomes a backdrop for public celebrations.

Simon-Bellamy House

Designed by the architect for his own family, this house is a renovation of a sad one-and-a-half-story bungalow in a New England coastal village dotted with glorious Victorian cottages and villas. To enlarge the original house so that it met the needs of a new family of three and still observed zoning restrictions, a second story was added, its height matching neighboring houses. A new tower at the house's front steals a water view blocked by houses across the street. The tower's curved mansard dome, recalling one atop a notable neighbor, joins with windows and stickwork at the front deck to become a giant ornament.

Inside, a hallway with tapering walls and ceiling extends down the center of the first floor, and appears much longer than it really is, making this small house (of about 2,000 square feet) seem grand. The family wanted many discrete places without the confinement of colonial houses, so alcove-like rooms are arranged along the hall. Each room offers a distinct surprise—the dining room has a shallow oval dome with grape lights, the living room waved ribbon panels, and the octagonal library a glittering dome of bicycle reflectors and mirrors. The greenhouse/conservatory is tiled, as is the kitchen, which along with the study has old wood cabinets. The hall terminates at the backyard, a park-like setting with large trees.

Upstairs the formality of the first floor is abandoned for personal requirements. The master bedroom has a sunning deck, a Thomas Jefferson bed, and stairs to the tower, a quiet place of contemplation and views. In the rear a child's bedroom has its own loft. Off the hall is a miniature laundry, and tiled bathroom with a skylight view of the tower dome.

Though this house has nostalgic moments, it is as new as its vinyl siding. It fondly recalls houses of the 19th century with 20th century requirements for economy of space and energy. It also proves that even small houses can have big dreams.

FIRST FLOOR   SECOND FLOOR

SECTION

OPPOSITE: Addition on former
one-story cottage features solar
panel tower.
Photo: Norman McGrath

LEFT: Living room is a spatial
event along house's corridor.
Photo: Norman McGrath

ABOVE: Library features domed
ceiling decorated with bicycle
reflectors.
Photo: Norman McGrath

$\mathcal{R}$owe House

This residence was designed to meet the requirements of a retired couple who owned land overlooking a quiet harbor on the Connecticut River. One of the clients is a gourmet cook who wanted a compact kitchen, open to entertaining spaces. Children and grandchildren visit occasionally, so a guestroom and bath were necessary. Also requested was a prominent entrance, so that friends might arrive through the front door, not the garage.

A careful manipulation of interior volumes enhances the feeling of spaciousness in this 2,000-square-foot house. The exposed roof rafters and cut-out hip beams give a broad, tent-like appearance to the roof, which rises from low eaves to a central tower at the entry vestibule. High windows in the tower admit light into the center of the house. The same broad roof texture extends over the entire main floor and deck which, because of the slope of the site, seems to sit high in the trees. The house is essentially invisible from the river side, which is stained the color of oak tree trunks, but bright and cheerful from the entry side—the color of a thousand daffodils planted in the forest.

The landscaping capitalizes on the natural features of the site. Rock ledge was uncovered and washed clean; cracks in the rocks were planted with thyme and other herbs. Instead of a lawn at the entry, the forest floor was reinforced with blueberry sod. The yellow lattice screen defines the entrance and wraps around to enclose a small secret garden, the only access to which is through the bedroom. A small swimming pool cut out of the ledge is surrounded by large rocks from the site and landscaped with evergreens and cotoneaster. It is surrounded by a lattice enclosure similar to that of the house, but painted the color of forest shadows. A tiny gazebo and deck overlook the river.

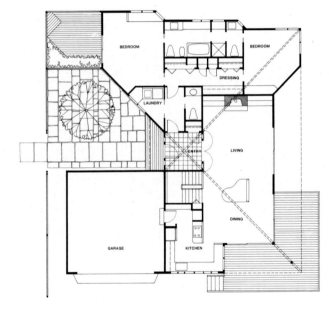

MAIN LEVEL

OPPOSITE: Front door is found under a welcoming archway.

Photo: Norman McGrath

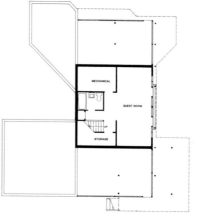

ABOVE: Privacy is protected by
trees and a lattice screen.
Photo: Norman McGrath

OPPOSITE: Interior is
distinguished by scalloped
clerestory dividers.
Photo: Norman McGrath

LOWER LEVEL

$\mathcal{W}$atkins Glen Master Plan and Seneca Lake Pier Pavilion

ABOVE: Master plan exploits the town's waterfront location on Seneca Lake.

OPPOSITE: Pier pavilion is a figural building that brings pier to terminus.

FLOOR PLAN

Watkins Glen, a small village in the Finger Lakes region of New York State, lies at the south end of the deepest lake in North America. Forty miles long and two miles wide, with hills cultivated in vineyards on either side, Seneca Lake provides for this village a fine natural panorama which the 19th century and early-20th century helped make a popular resort. In the 1970s, however, Watkins Glen fell into decline. In 1980, a local public agency, citing rising unemployment, a falling population, and deepening economic depression, cast about for a way to turn around the county's troubled economy. The agency settled on renewed tourism as the most feasible route to prosperity, but a challenging one. The lakefront offered Schuyler County its best hope. Here, village streets came tantalizingly close to water views of extraordinary beauty, only to be blocked by rusting cars and industrial detritus.

The first task was to create a physical plan for the waterfront. This was completed in 1981, with a televised design workshop involving many of the region's residents, as had been previously done by Centerbrook in Roanoke, Virginia. Waterfront land was acquired from Conrail for a public park. The first project planned for the park was a fishing pier with a pavilion at its end, designed to act as the principal symbol for Watkins Glen and to provide public access to its lakefront.

The pier is 330 feet long. Its special details, such as shipboard "wire" lights, are meant to communicate a maritime character that the waterfront heretofore lacked. The pavilion's architecture refers to Adirondack boathouses and also the Victorian architecture of Watkins Glen, but it is the refinement of these idioms into a simple, symmetrical structure with a memorable silhouette that is meant to give the pavilion its symbolic character.

"Timespell"

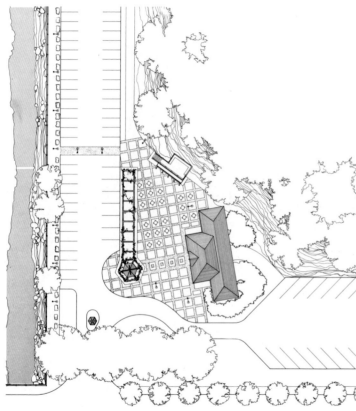

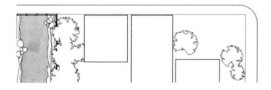

OPPOSITE, FROM TOP: Park structures become beacons drawing night visitors.

Natural gorge becomes the canvas for a laser light multi-media show.

Located on Franklin Street near the best resort hotels, the Watkins Glen State Park, a spectacular 1.4-mile-long natural gorge, has been the village's and the region's principal attraction for nearly a century. By the 1980s, however, the village of Watkins Glen was becoming dilapidated as was the State Park.

A development plan for Watkins Glen and the surrounding county suggested that a strengthened State Park, with a more appealing and commodious Visitor's Center, could become the linchpin of a renewed Finger Lakes tourism industry. Of prime importance in this master plan was an idea for transforming the State Park into a nighttime attraction in order to create an inducement to visitors to extend their stay in Watkins Glen.

It was decided that a special sound and light show could be built into a widening of the walls of the Watkins Glen Gorge, where there was space for about 500 people. The show, called "Timespell," tells the story of the 450-billion-year history of the gorge from the first moments of the earth's origins to modern time. The show is computer-controlled, with extensive lighting stations and other technical hardware hidden from view to ensure maintenance of a natural environment for hikers during the day.

The entrance to the park is opened up to view from Franklin Street and is organized into a grouping of pavilions. An important objective for these pavilions is the creation of an architecture that looks sufficiently rustic by day that the park visitor is comfortable, yet, like the gorge itself, an architecture that has a theatrical nighttime presence. Many of the shades and colors of the new State Park architecture—and also of its two dimensional ornamentation, are derived from traditional designs of the Seneca Indians, one of the five tribes of the Iroquois Nation and the earliest known civilization to inhabit the gorge.

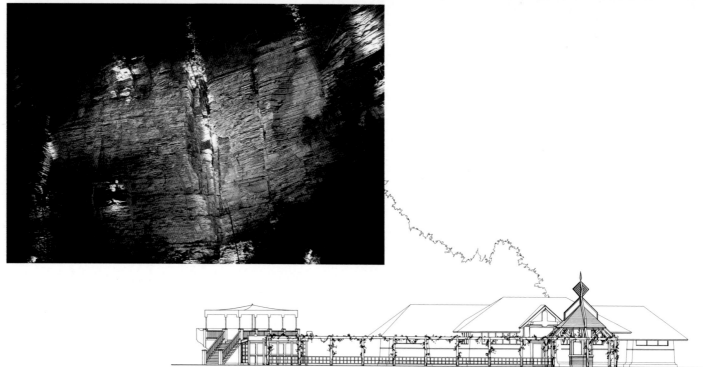

$\mathcal{L}$enz Winery

ABOVE: Sloping trellis with vines reduces the scale of the barn.
Photo: Norman McGrath

OPPOSITE: Trellises and landscaping unify building around the courtyard.
Photo: Norman McGrath

A former Long Island potato farm transformed into an appropriate setting in which to bottle and market wine, this vineyard and winery is open to the public and wholesalers. The clients, who cherish their privacy, live on the farm. They asked that the winery signal its presence with an entry gate. Cars were to be kept out of sight of the house, the existing pool made private, and the commercial elements kept within an existing barn.

The design task was primarily one of landscape and exterior reorganization. Inexpensive pressure-treated "peeler" poles (also used as the vineyard stakes) are used for trellises throughout the project to create a sense of procession. At the road front the trellises become an arch entry which can close if traffic requires. Covered with fox grape, the trellised entry offers symbolic recognition for the vineyard.

Once through the gate, visitors drive through the grape rows to park at a second entry—an outdoor hall carved from the unused center bay of an old garage. Tapering to a narrow three feet, this pedestrian entry heightens expectations as one enters a court. Here, more trellises across from the garage complete a formal courtyard.

To ease the expansive front of the barn, trellises are employed again, arching up to make clear to the public which door of its many is the entry. Inside, the east wing of the barn serves as a garage for tractors, the west wing as the winery itself, and the north shed as the cask room. The central room, carefully restored, is for visitors. The large space allows for an indoor stencilled folly that separates the wine display area from a tasting room and serves as a sales counter and bar for large receptions.

At one end of the garage is an animal shed that now houses gray geese and goats. At the rear of the house a deck casually overlooks the court where the vintners relax, enjoying their homestead.

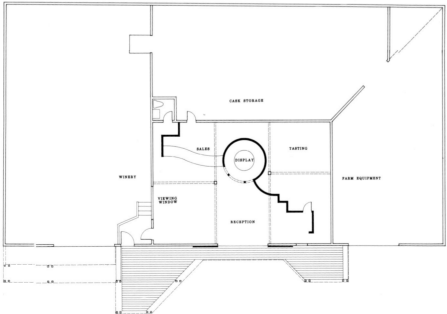

ABOVE: Rustic structure serves as a ceremonial gate to the winery.
Photo: Norman McGrath

OPPOSITE: Freestanding partition divides sales and tasting area.
Photo: Norman McGrath

Elliott House

ABOVE: The house appears as a village of similar forms.
Photo: William Robinson

RIGHT: Entry is behind the screen wall, and under a trellis.
Photo: Norman McGrath

OPPOSITE: At night, the house appears mysterious and whimsical.
Photo: William Robinson

This solar-heated house was designed for an artist, her writer husband, and their young daughter. Sited on the crest of a hill, it commands a view to the south of the Laurel Highlands in western Pennsylvania. The surrounding hills, cleared into farmland and crossed by fences, recall the magical highlands of Scotland and are a fitting home for the hounds and horsemen of the famed Rolling Rock Hunt.

The house is a complex of three individual buildings—an art studio, a writer's cottage, and the main house, which contains an art gallery and library wing. The buildings align with the edge of a forest where it meets an open field of wheat and, in some places, step back from the tree line. A garden wall provides alignment with the trees and creates an outdoor corridor connecting the separate buildings. Openings in the garden wall set a rhythm which focuses on an old split rail fence at the center of the complex. This fence was the owner's favorite destination on her walks as a young girl among these hills, and it is now the symbolic heart of the house.

While the wheat fields extend up to the south wall of the house, the hunt trail cuts through the woods just to the north of the house, where a stepped deck provides spectator seating for the equestrian event. Windows in the art studio and writer's cottage face each other across a small semi-circular clearing in the trees.

Inside, native woods used for the floors, cabinets, and ceilings combine with the plastered wall, soap stone, and slate tiles and a palette of rich greens, oranges, and browns (derived from favorite passages of Dashiell Hammett's *The Dain Curse*) to create an exotic setting in harmony with the literary and artistic work of the owners and their imagined habitation of abodes deep within enchanted forests.

LEFT TOP: Entry is gained through a greenhouse enclosure.
Photo: Norman McGrath

ABOVE: Entry hall wall is imprinted with leaves pressed into wet plaster.
Photo: Norman McGrath

LEFT: Library offers a small cozy space for reading.
Photo: Norman McGrath

OPPOSITE: House's south side holds open porches and a bedroom tower.
Photo: Norman McGrath

FIRST FLOOR

SECOND FLOOR

Cape Cod Cottage

ABOVE: Exterior sports materials native to New England coast.
Photo: Joanne Devereaux

OPPOSITE: Pine clad interior exudes warmth and vacation cabin esthetic.
Photo: Joanne Devereaux

Two couples, the joint owners of a 400-square-foot garage on a commanding Cape Cod site, wanted to transform their modest property into a vacation home complete with kitchen, eating area, sleeping space for six, and a full bath. The budget was $20,000, including architectural fees.

Although space was to be at a minimum, the owners desired an airiness and informality appropriate to the seashore. A palette of bright colors was used in combination with pine beadboard, a material redolent with seaside cottage atmosphere. Many of the original garage elements were retained, including an overhead door whose panels were replaced with glass to make a large window. On warm days the garage door can be opened to bring the outside in, while a roll-up screen keeps insects out.

Wood French doors with curtains make the bedroom private. But when the doors are open, their five-foot width enlarges both bedroom and living area. To sleep six, a loft for two was tucked over the kitchen, and the living area has a fold-out couch for two more.

An outside space amidst an adjacent tall pine grove is provided with a 200-square-foot deck. From it, a ship's ladder climbs to a widow's walk which looks out on a panorama of the Atlantic, set against a foreground of salt marshes and ponds. An old Coast Guard station stands watch over a barrier sand dune.

This little seashore retreat, resurrected from an unused garage, has become a useful vacation house. Future plans call for expanding the deck to accommodate a six-person tent that will enable the two families to enjoy the house simultaneously.

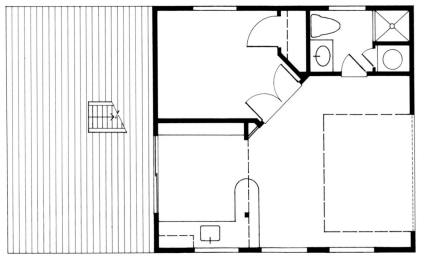

FIRST FLOOR

Crowell Studio

This ocean retreat is a composer's studio in the Hampton dunes. Though it adjoins a permanent residence next door, it is large enough to serve as a vacation house.

Reminiscent of Long Island windmills and lighthouses, an octagonal tower domed with lead-coated copper is the building's core. Hip roofs slope off the tower to the north, protecting it from winter winds. Large double-hung windows face south to gain the sun's warmth. Roofs and walls are of red cedar shingles, and cedar lattice-work abounds in rails and porch overhangs.

Codes required that the house be built on pilings, with the first floor 11 feet above sea level. A cedar lattice skirt hides the pilings and protects non-habitable storage areas on grade. This skirt becomes a railing for the long ambling stair that leads to the front door and expands into a small sunning deck.

From the deck one enters a studio/living room carpeted for acoustics. Big enough for both a grand piano and sitting area, it has three "piano key" skylights which illuminate the composer's work space without allowing direct sunlight on the instrument. The focus of the studio/living room is a wide set of steps under a tall arch that leads to the bedroom, and a second set of rambling stairs. These narrow and steep stairs lead to a tower room, surrounded like a lighthouse by windows and a walkway (requested by the musician to pace while composing). The tower room's space extends up under the dome. High at the top is a cupola for light.

The success of this house lies in its rambling seaside spirit. Designed with romantic gesture, it fondly remembers old and fast-disappearing Long Island neighbors. Even so, it makes no pretense of belonging to any but its own time.

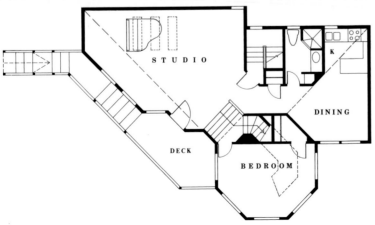

ABOVE: Structure has the
bearing of a miniature
lighthouse.
Photo: Timothy Hursley

RIGHT: A crooked stair climbs
to composing studio.
Photo: Timothy Hursley

OPPOSITE: A secluded room at
tower top has its own
promenade deck.
Photo: Timothy Hursley

*C*ampus Master Plan/
Residence Hall "Suntraps"

Centerbrook has been the architect for Quinnipiac College since 1977, when a campus-wide master plan was developed with the active participation of the entire college community. The plan does not locate specific future building projects, but rather defines a concept to guide the preliminary design and siting of buildings and renovations as the college's needs develop and fund raising efforts progress.

One of the first projects undertaken, "suntraps," dealt solely with the spaces between existing buildings rather than the buildings themselves. The suntraps encompass an eighth-mile stretch of road along which most of the dormitories are located. One of the goals of the master plan was to create a lively village street out of the then rather bleak and barren dorm road. The scheme makes use of small piazzas with drinking fountains, orchards of Bradford Pear trees which blossom very early in Spring when the students are still on campus, tables and benches located along the sidewalk of the street (which is the main pedestrian path to the classrooms), and a series of suntraps— south-facing enclaves enclosed by masonry walls which trap the sun while providing protection from the wind. The suntraps create outdoor gathering places which are habitable even in fall and winter, which is, after all, when the students are in session. The result is a setting which is at once bucolic and urbane, where friends see each other, exchange hellos, gather informally, and enjoy their community.

ABOVE: Catching the setting sun, campus proscenium is a backdrop for campus events.
Photo: Jeff Goldberg/Esto

OPPOSITE: South-facing plaza's masonry walls invite sun-worshipers.
Photo: Norman McGrath

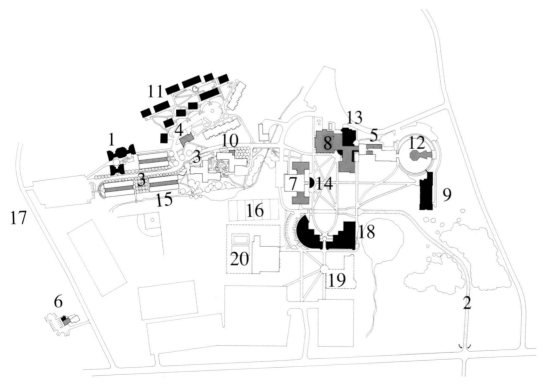

LEGEND

1 Student Apartment Complex 1979
2 New Entry Gate and Road 1982
3 Suntraps 1984
4 Student Affairs Offices 1984
5 Computer Center 1982-1985
6 Alumni House 1985
7 Administrative Offices 1986
8 Dining Hall and Servery 1986-1988
9 Echlin Health Sciences Center 1989
10 Security Office 1990
11 Residence Hall Village 1991
12 Clarice L. Buckman Theater 1990
13 Carl Hansen Student Center 1991
14 Quadrangle Proscenium 1991
15 Business School (under construction)
16 Recreation Center addition (under construction)
17 Athletic Fields (under construction)
18 Law School (in design)
19 Renovation of Alumni Hall (in design)
20 Renovation of Allied Health Facilities (in design)
21 Addition to Library (in design)
22 New Residence Hall (in design)

*E*chlin Health Sciences Center

Quinnipiac College
Hamden, Connecticut

By its program alone, this Health Sciences Center was to be an ordinary academic building, consisting of classrooms, seminar rooms, a lecture hall, and faculty offices. However, the college requested that it fulfill two other goals. The first was to consider the building itself as a teacher. To this end, the building was made an attraction to students with the provision of interior windows looking in from the hallways to the robotics and therapy laboratories, so that students could view the offerings inside. The building also provides a social setting with a variety of lounges set along the hallway edges, like plazas on a street, where students and professors can meet and exchange ideas informally and spontaneously.

The second goal was to simultaneously relate the new building to an adjacent and somewhat undistinguished one-story circular building and to complete the formation of the central campus by relating the new building to the library, located some 600 feet to the east. The solution, in part, was to connect the circular building with a brick archway. In this way, the one-story facade of the circular building takes on the appearance and stature of a low garden wall. The archway creates a threshold separating the parking area to the south from the newly created courtyard. The new building extends in a north/south orientation to enclose the west side of campus. A large gabled roof, positioned over the main entrance to the center, is set on axis with the library bell tower. The new Board of Trustees room is housed on the second floor under the gabled roof, providing, upon entering the room, a panoramic view of the campus with its signature bell tower at the focal point.

Building defines west edge of campus quadrangle.
Photo: Norman McGrath

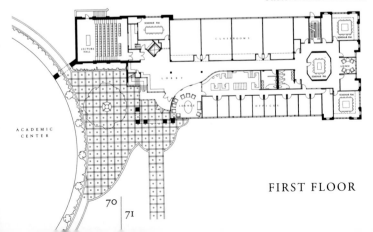

FIRST FLOOR

70
71

*C*omputer Center

This space was converted from three adjacent classrooms. The center room houses the central processing offices, faculty and supervisor's offices, an environmentally sealed computer room, and a computer laboratory for student instruction. Conceived as part of the overall master plan, which reinforces the image of the college as a village, the computer center is viewed from the corridor like a store on Main Street. The computer room announces itself along the corridor with brightly tiled and windowed protrusions that provide tantalizing views of the central computer and beyond into the student laboratories. The laboratory itself can be viewed from the corridor through its own display window exhibiting its CRT stations in a curved, two-level array. A curved wall blocks glare from exterior windows and is adorned with a computer-generated garland hand-stenciled by the architects. The passing students, like window shoppers, are thus introduced to the offerings of the computer curriculum.

Center has two levels of computer stations with indirect lighting.
Photo: Norman McGrath

*D*ining Hall and Servery

Quinnipiac College
Hamden, Connecticut

The college's desire to invest in an asset salable to prospective students, and to make better use of the dining facility, which was one of the largest single spaces on campus and perhaps the most underutilized, created the need for a complete renovation of an existing dining hall and servery.

Because it is tied into the main stream of traffic with the Student Union at the intersection of the academic and residential halves of the campus, the dining hall has become a social center for not only those purchasing food, but also for casual gatherings and entertainment. Informal performances take place at the proscenium end of the dining hall, which is framed by stairs descending from balconies offering views through new clerestory windows of Sleeping Giant State Park. The balcony rails provide prominent billboards for display of banners announcing various campus events. A variety of spaces is created by the use of these balconies: some are large and open, others are small with low ceilings. A low-ceilinged "cafe" overlooks the pedestrian activity on the college's main pathway. Private dining rooms on the mezzanine level can be opened for general use or shut off from the rest of the dining area for privacy.

ABOVE: Entry to dining hall is through dramatic two-story space.
Photo: Jeff Goldberg/Esto

LEFT: Dining area allows views of adjacent state park.
Photo: Paul Warchol

OPPOSITE: Bright colors and curved forms give space its dynamism.
Photo: Paul Warchol

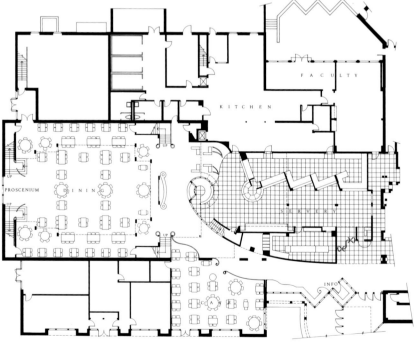

LOWER LEVEL

Carl Hansen Student Center

Quinnipiac College
Hamden, Connecticut

ABOVE: Second level above rotunda overlook glass-block curved wall.
Photo: Jeff Goldberg/Esto

OPPOSITE, TOP: Rotunda provides a central meeting place for students.
Photo: Jeff Goldberg/Esto

OPPOSITE, BOTTOM: Southeast entry to student center is marked by glass-block wall.
Photo: Jeff Goldberg/Esto

This new student center transforms an existing student center, giving it a sociability and verve that it previously lacked, as well as doubling its size. The new center connects with the renovated dining hall and servery, the main classroom building, and the Alumni Hall multi-purpose room.

The existing hallway leading from the dining hall to the classrooms, which passed through the existing student center, was maintained and enlivened along its full length with elements of village life which contribute to a sense of well-being and sociability. A small cafe and reading lounge flank the hallway before it expands to form an indoor agora, ringed by an abstracted forest of "trees" which offer their curvilinear "roots" as places to sit. At this "town center" are a bookstore, post office, bank, and convenience store.

A large sculptural "tree" in the middle of the agora suggests the historic Charter Oak, symbol of both the college and the state of Connecticut, whose branches reach upward to the second floor, and cast down a canopy of leaves in the form of irregularly sized green-tinted glass blocks, set within a curved, south-facing wall. This wall introduces sunlight into the previously dark interior of the student center and allows access to a small outdoor suntrap, where a curved sitting wall invites students to lounge beneath a spreading magnolia tree. Upstairs, a chapel, radio station, game room, music listening room, and student locker area face onto the hallway to continue the village square theme set below.

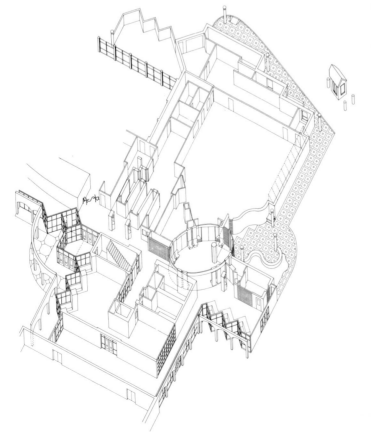

$\mathcal{R}$esidence Hall Village

Quinnipiac College
Hamden, Connecticut

This complex of 11 separate residence halls houses 336 students in six-person suites. The buildings were planned to gracefully climb the steep hillside site with a minimum of disturbance to the existing contours. They are also intended to create small neighborhoods and allow the students to assign identities to each house, such as the "French House" or "Non-Smokers House." A single exterior entry door for each house (desirable for security reasons) opens into a vestibule, from which four apartments are then entered. A laundry room located in each vestibule provides a place for the residents in each house to meet casually, much as the town well did in another era.

The economical repetition of a single building design is obscured by combining the front sides, back sides, and gable ends of the buildings to form courtyards. Occasionally, two buildings are joined together to form one. Brick walls with arched openings connect the buildings and create a variety of small courtyards, each with a special ambiance of its own. One is shaded by a large tree encircled by a low sitting wall; another faces east and receives the early morning sun; another commands a panoramic view of Sleeping Giant State Park to the north. Although numerous steps are required to climb the hillside, gently ramping paths connecting with landings and terraces make every building fully accessible.

SITE PLAN

EXISTING DORM

EXISTING REC BLDG

EXISTING DORM

EXISTING DORM

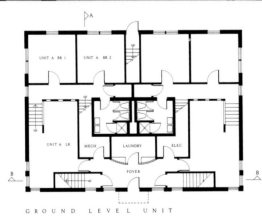

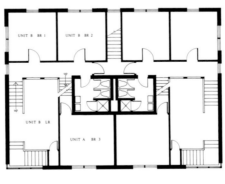

UNIT A BR 1	UNIT A BR 2

UNIT A LR	MECH	LAUNDRY	ELEC

FOYER

GROUND LEVEL UNIT

UNIT B BR 1	UNIT B BR 2

UNIT B LR

UNIT A BR 3

UPPER LEVEL UNIT

TYPICAL FLOOR PLAN

UNIT B BR 3

UPPER LEVEL UNIT

ABOVE LEFT: Dormitories negotiate a sloped site with curved stairs and walls.
Photo: Jeff Goldberg/Esto

ABOVE RIGHT: Connecting archways give site a layered quality.
Photo: Jeff Goldberg/Esto

OPPOSITE: Low walls and archways create private courtyards between buildings.
Photo: Jeff Goldberg/Esto

$\mathcal{P}$rivate Library

The client for this renovation of a foyer, dining room, and library/writing studio in a duplex apartment wanted an interior elegant enough for the most glamourous of friends, yet comfortable and efficient for her daily work of putting words to paper. She also desired architecture of invention, superior craftsmanship, and lasting value—something on a par with her extraordinary antiques.

Located below the upper penthouse floor, which is glassy and light, these new spaces offer a counterpoint—a vaulted retreat—a place to dine on cold winter nights and to work year-round, hidden away from the world.

Within a shell of uninspired, boxey spaces, new ceilings, cabinets, and columns were created from teak. These are rendered in an invented classic style, inspired by visions of libraries by H.H. Richardson and an imagined but nonexistent English Renaissance. Teak allows high relief. Its color is warm, but has a slight green cast that accentuates its modeling and the craft of the cabinetmaker. Deep terra-cotta red walls contrast with the teak. Lighting is hidden in the column capitals to give the ceilings a soft glow at night.

At the center of the three spaces is a staircase with Art Nouveau like wrought iron railings leading up to the penthouse. A few shallow steps at the window end of the library lead up to a raised floor—a platform for reading and interviewing with a view of Central Park below. Desks and bookshelves are designed with great care. Some drawers are shallow with felt liners and folding metal rods to hold down loose stacks of typed pages. These allow the writer to be able to close up shop at a moment's notice for an unexpected visitor.

Designed to withstand the whims of an inveterate collector, the interior has its own distinctive character, enough to meld eclectic origins and become a remarkable place of its own.

THIS PAGE: Wood clad columns and ceiling offer space an air of permanence.
Photo: Timothy Hursley

OPPOSITE: Writing study is sheltered by gently arching ceiling.
Photo: Timothy Hursley

*H*ood Museum of Art

ABOVE: Contemporary art gallery is a soaring space filled with large works.
Photo: Steve Rosenthal

OPPOSITE: Hood is found between Wilson Hall to left and Hopkins Center.
Photo: Timothy Hursley

The Hood Museum of Art strengthens education in the arts at Dartmouth College, which first came into its own in 1962 with completion of the Hopkins Center for the Performing Arts, designed by Wallace K. Harrison. At 39,000 square feet, the Hood Museum adds to the Hopkins Center a building dedicated solely to the fine arts. The Hood has 12 art galleries; a 222-seat film and lecture theater; storage, work, and administration spaces; plus connectors to several adjacent buildings—notably Harrison's modernist performing arts center and a Romanesque building, Wilson Hall, that has been renovated into performing arts classrooms. The museum building program required an individual identity for the museum, but it asked also for connection to these two flanking structures in order to ensure student exposure to all the arts, and to reduce the effect of inclement weather in this northern climate.

The museum was configured north-south along the east edge of the site in order to create a wall that might hide the heating plant. In the resulting space between the museum and the Hopkins Center, several small courtyards—an idea new to Dartmouth—were created with two connectors. Pedestrian circulation is maintained from courtyard to courtyard along a gently ramped path. The museum's turned gable roof and simple brick walls are reminiscent of traditional New England architecture.

Inside, the galleries are subordinated to the objects on exhibit. A series of small galleries aligned along the longitudinal axis of the building are reminiscent of the public rooms of great houses for which many of the objects were originally intended. A 20th century gallery on the top floor has high walls for the display of large works.

LEFT: Monumental stair leads from museum entry to contemporary gallery.
Photo: Steve Rosenthal

BELOW: Smaller galleries are found adjacent to larger ones.
Photo: Steve Rosenthal

OPPOSITE, TOP AND LEFT: Brick blends with adjacent vault-roofed Hopkins Center.
Photo: Timothy Hursley

OPPOSITE, RIGHT: Courtyard is accessed through the entry portals.
Photo: Steve Rosenthal

ABOVE: Entry courtyard
is a quiet, protected
space.
Photo: Steve Rosenthal

OPPOSITE: Bright colors
and light greet visitors
in entry lobby.
Photo: Steve Rosenthal

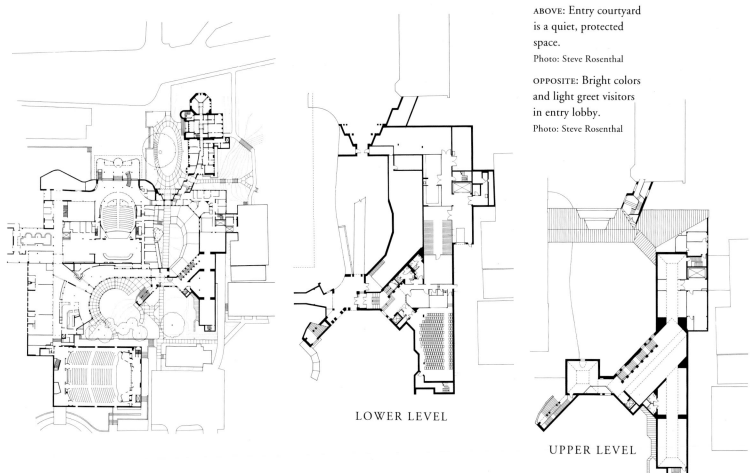

LOWER LEVEL

UPPER LEVEL

ℬaldwin House

The client for this house, a widower in his sixties, had lived most of his life in a rather dark house and longed for high open spaces and ample sunlight. This 1,500-square-foot house fulfills his wish for open space, because it is essentially one large room with a central fireplace, convertible into three. Two corners of the large space can be closed for a bedroom and guestroom/study, respectively. Lots of south-facing glass, shaded in summer by a huge sugar maple, allows the sun to warm the house during the winter months. The warm air heating system circulates the solar heated air to the two corner rooms on the house's north side. A semi-detached garage has a large attic and workshop, as well as the heating/airconditioning systems.

The house is sited on a small lot, facing a quiet village street, bounded on the north and south by stone walls. There is a view to the south of a lovely New England cemetery, and here was placed a stone terrace for privacy. Landscaping consists of natural rocks on the site, Boston ivy ground cover, grass, and several varieties of evergreens, used as screening from adjacent properties.

Many of the materials are part of the New England building vernacular: wood frame construction, cedar clapboard siding, brick and stone chimneys, and oversized double-hung windows. A wood-burning stove can heat the entire house. The exterior is shades of green against natural stone walls, with chimney accents of red brick. Interior colors are warm terra-cotta, brick, grays, and occasional accents of plum and purple. Guestroom and bedroom walls are covered with felt to provide an acoustic dampening from the large room.

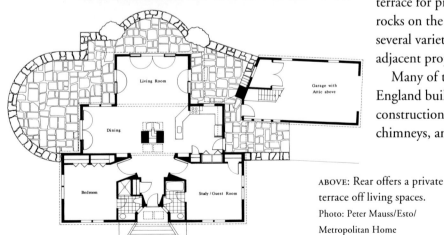

ABOVE: Rear offers a private terrace off living spaces.
Photo: Peter Mauss/Esto/Metropolitan Home

OPPOSITE: Light filled interior is dominated by chimney mass.
Photo: Peter Mauss/Esto/Metropolitan Home

Samuel's Clothing Store

High drama and theatrical flair characterize this women's clothing store in a suburban shopping mall. In order to keep up with fashion's seasonal changes in style, color, and material, the interior can be visually altered. This is accomplished through the use of 120 theater fixtures with changing gels in conjunction with a

ABOVE AND OPPOSITE:
Stage lighting and central turntable give interior theatrical atmosphere.
Photos: Norman McGrath

computerized dimmer board that modulates each light's intensity, giving great flexibility to the changing interior.

A neutral gray carpet background provides a screen on which the color gels work warm or cool, changing the atmosphere and the mood only through the lighting. Dark blue columns seem weightier for their color.

Everything in this store has been designed to move, or to give the illusion of movement, with the least amount of effort. Even the four large dressing rooms, made of mirror-clad plywood and pipe railing, move around the store on wheels.

In the center of the showroom is a custom-made turntable with variable speeds, on which changing displays are synchronized with the computer to be highlighted at different moments. A bright yellow MG sports car, a speedboat, even an Ultralight have rested on the turntable, complete with extravagantly dressed mannequins who, with the help of changing light, seem to wave to passersby.

$\mathcal{A}$ndrews House

This Victorian-era brick house was designed in 1872 by Josiah Cleveland Cady, who also designed the original Metropolitan Opera House in New York City. Rooms in the existing house are formal and elegant but are also small and separate from each other. The clients asked for a large room that would be the major space for day-to-day living in the house.

The new room, adjacent and opening to the kitchen, accommodates a small dining table, seating around a fireplace, television, and books. An alcove provides space for a small office, and French doors open onto the lawn. The octagonal plan organizes both circulation and vistas in the space. Three windows and the opening to the kitchen occupy four sides of the octagon; three doorways and the fireplace complete the shape. The lantern and the northwest skylight provide balanced light for both the new room and the kitchen. The lantern windows afford comfortable summer ventilation. In the winter, concealed fans move warm air from the lantern down into the main part of the room.

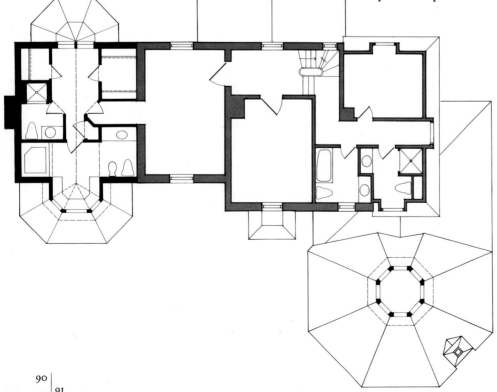

Octagonal and bay window wing additions blend with late 19th century original.
Photo: Courtesy of *House Beautiful*, the Hearst Corporation, all rights reserved.

ABOVE: Octagonal room draws additional light and height from shallow domed ceiling.

Photo: Courtesy of *House Beautiful*, the Hearst Corporation, all rights reserved.

OPPOSITE: South-facing terrace can be viewed from octagonal addition.

Photo: Courtesy of *House Beautiful*, the Hearst Corporation, all rights reserved.

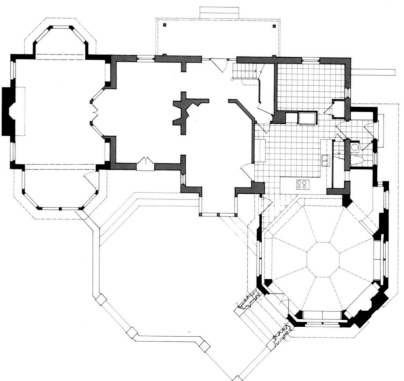

Student Center

The Trustees of this private college, in the wake of their decision to abolish on-campus fraternities, commissioned a 28,000-square-foot student center to provide a new focus for academic social life. It was to be a sociable building, offering students and faculty a variety of lounges and meeting rooms, and had to be truly multi-purpose in its function. Students, teachers, and other members of the university community participated in an on-site design workshop to help define the new building's role.

While the site chosen by Centerbrook—on a major path that connects the two halves of the campus—was ideal for a building that was to become the social center of the college, it also posed the risk of dividing rather than unifying the campus. The solution was to make the building bridge the path and thus become a gateway linking both sides of the campus not only physically but symbolically as well.

Approaching from the north side, which is faced in red brick to match other campus buildings, one passes through the gateway to a south-facing terrace. White clapboard walls spread out to shield this enclave from the prevailing north winds and to collect the warmth of the sun. From here one enters into the main lobby where the post office, newsstand, bank, activities desk, and post office lounge are grouped.

Off the main lobby is the multi-purpose room, a large space for parties, dinners, lectures, concerts, seminars, and meetings. The room is ringed with balconies set behind free-standing facades, creating the sense of an intimate space suited to small groups of people while, in fact, the room can accommodate up to 800. The balconies can be converted to meeting and activity rooms for student clubs and seminar groups when they are not being used for large-scale events.

OPPOSITE TOP: Materials
and color relate to existing
campus buildings
Photo: Norman McGrath

OPPOSITE BOTTOM: The
center creates a gateway for
pedestrian traffic.
Photo: Norman McGrath

ABOVE: Window in bridge
looks out over campus.
Photo: Norman McGrath

ABOVE RIGHT: Multi-
purpose room interior
appears as a village within
the building.
Photo: Norman McGrath

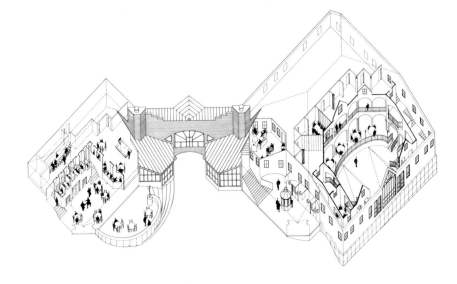

East Hampton Library and Community Center

Located in a small, central Connecticut mill town, this community center houses a library, day care, and senior center. Three community agencies joined their facilities to enrich occupants and limit costs. Sharing more than just a roof and mechanical systems, the three parts mutually use kitchens, staff rooms, and a meeting hall. Nonetheless, each agency wanted its own identity. Local citizens became a crucial part of the design process. A diverse committee of 35 residents collaborated in a series of design workshops that initially focused on the site and user needs.

The site is complex. Laid out on an east-west axis, the building opens to south light and averts the cold with long roofs. The smallest component, the senior center, is closest to the road and sized to match residential buildings nearby. Day care is at the center, and the library is at the rear. This stepped plan gives all three parts equal recognition from the street.

Each facility locates activities along the porch and at entries so that passersby are urged to visit. A community bulletin board and a view of children's crafts welcomes library users. Seniors can sit indoors or out to enjoy the passing scene. The day care center is always on view, and so is the seniors' store.

The building is designed to harmonize with its small village surroundings and evoke pride in the citizenry. Townspeople and architects stencilled bell patterns at entries and at the library, recalling the town's heritage as "Belltown" (the original home of America's bell manufacturing). The family of chimney, ventilator, and bell towers spire high as civic markers, while windows and dormers give a friendly cadence to the building's substantial mass.

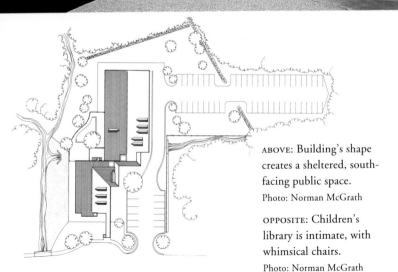

ABOVE: Building's shape creates a sheltered, south-facing public space.
Photo: Norman McGrath

OPPOSITE: Children's library is intimate, with whimsical chairs.
Photo: Norman McGrath

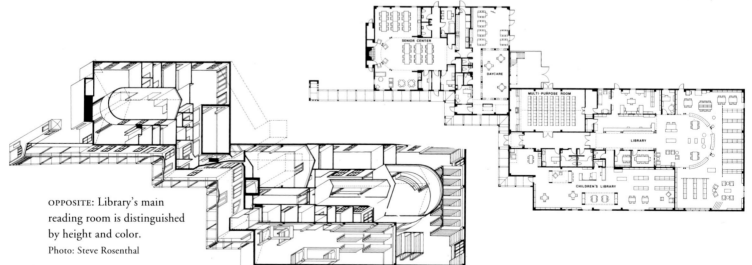

OPPOSITE: Library's main reading room is distinguished by height and color.
Photo: Steve Rosenthal

ABOVE LEFT: Columns, overhangs, and door's bell stenciling create an intimate scale.
Photo: Norman McGrath

ABOVE RIGHT: Apse end of library is comfortable sitting area.
Photo: Norman McGrath

*W*illiams College Museum of Art

ABOVE: Addition recalls
geometry and materials of
original building.
Photo: Steve Rosenthal

OPPOSITE: Restored rotunda
of original museum, with
galleries beyond.
Photo: Steve Rosenthal

The expansion of this college museum was a complex undertaking. The building is used by several different groups of people: museum visitors, art history students, artists, faculty, and administrators. The existing museum was housed in a series of handsome rooms axially disposed about a columned rotunda (originally the college library), designed by Thomas Tefft of Providence in 1846. It has been renovated to accommodate the demands of a modern museum without changing its character.

The additions address each of the program aspects. The atrium, built on level ground south of the existing building, acts as a transitional space that is open to all building users. Museum galleries on the top floor and offices on the entry floor are easily closed off and made secure when the museum is closed. On the lower level, a large classroom is accessible for daytime or evening lectures, while the more private realms of slide-room and faculty offices can be closed during the evening. At the lowest level of the building service space can be entered directly from outside for maximum flexibility of use.

The new museum spaces on the top floor of the building are organized about an axis that extends south from the original rotunda through a small square gallery, across a long rectangular gallery, through the atrium on a bridge, and finally into the octagonal end of the new main gallery. The shape of the new gallery recalls the oldest part of the building, while the expansive floor space, unbroken walls, and skylighted spaces offer all the facilities of a modern gallery.

The character of the exterior is in keeping with its surroundings. Materials include brick and stucco with white wood trim, all in the spirit of the original building.

OPPOSITE, FROM TOP:
Subdued gallery with art enhanced by dark colors.
Photo: Steve Rosenthal

Bridge offers multiple views of entry atrium.
Photo: Steve Rosenthal

THIS PAGE: Double-height space is enlivened with multi-level circulation.
Photo: Norman McGrath

THE NEW ENGLAND EYE

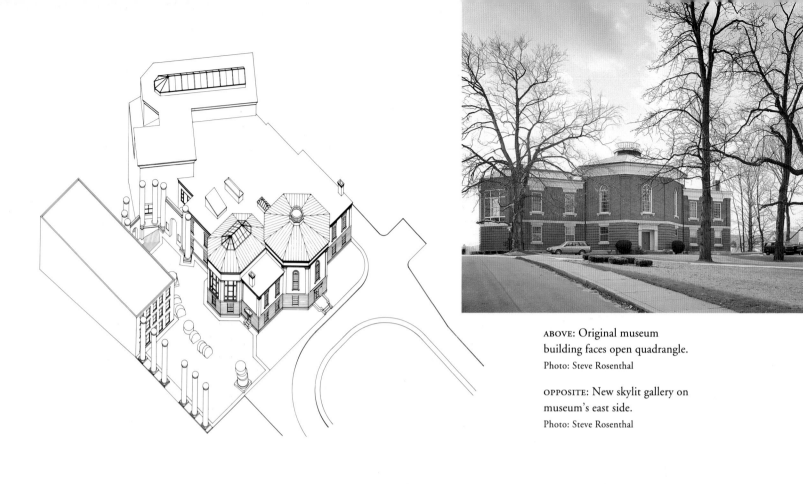

ABOVE: Original museum building faces open quadrangle.
Photo: Steve Rosenthal

OPPOSITE: New skylit gallery on museum's east side.
Photo: Steve Rosenthal

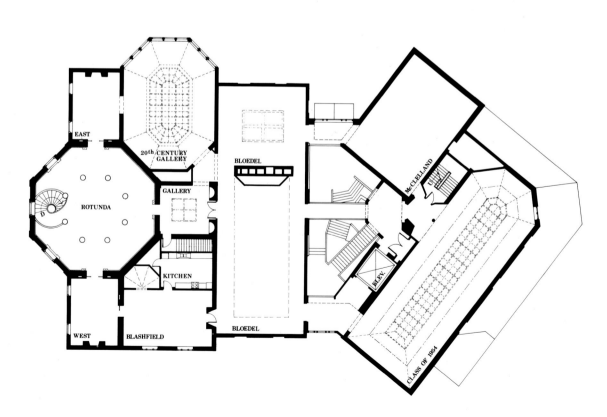

ℛeid House I

ABOVE: Living room receives
light from windows and
skylights over fireplace.
Photo: Peter Mauss/Esto

OPPOSITE: Illuminated at
night, the house yields its
secrets.
Photo: Peter Mauss/Esto

This house takes its place among the stately, turn-of-the-century houses of this Cleveland suburb. Situated on a one-acre site with neighbors close by on three sides, and a heavily traveled street on the fourth, the house completes the enclosure of a fenced courtyard. By passing through an arched gate in the courtyard fence, one leaves behind the busy, public world of neighbors and street to find a private, gardened courtyard.

From the courtyard one enters the house. Care was given to make the organization of the various parts of the house easy to understand and memorable. This was done in two ways: First, a path connecting one end of the house to the other was created, along which all the rooms are arranged. A curving, colorful display wall and a large, tree-shaped hall window are landmarks along the way. Second, the house is divided internally into two clearly identifiable districts, public and private, with interior windows looking down from the private realm of second floor bedrooms to the public spaces of living room, entry, dining room, and den.

The house's design is intended to evoke emotional responses from its inhabitants by manipulating space and light so that constrained spaces release into expanded ones, views look down from above and up from below, sun floods the kitchen in the morning and the living room in the evening, and dramatic vistas of the tree tops are viewed through windows set high in the peaks of the dormers. Additionally, special places are provided for the display of the owners' collections of art and objects brought back from their travels.

OPPOSITE: Beyond the gate,
interior courtyard is an ordered
outdoor room.
Photo: Peter Mauss/Esto

LEFT: Curved wall in dining
room offers niches for art
display.
Photo: Peter Mauss/Esto

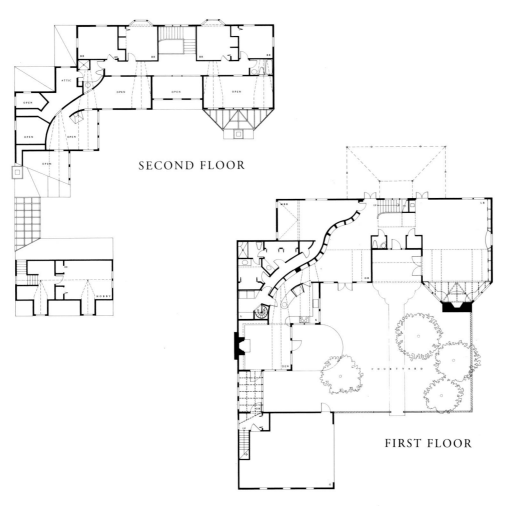

SECOND FLOOR

FIRST FLOOR

$\mathcal{M}$cKim House

ABOVE: Elliptical living room
has stickwork cornice and
mantle.
Photo: Timothy Hursley

OPPOSITE: Free-standing
gables shelter portals and
balcony.
Photo: Timothy Hursley

This vacation home enjoys a high, windswept site on
Fisher's Island that looks north across a sound to the
Connecticut shoreline. Approached from the west, it
appears as a tribe of connected buildings, a brood of
structures surrounding a mother house, sharing a family
resemblance in their cedar shingle siding, dark gable
roofs, and random "crazy quilt" stickwork. The porte
cochere (created by the extension of the storage shed's
roof over the driveway) leads to a small gravel court
where the main house faces a "drunken" fence to the
south. The house's gabled, court face has windows all
likewise gabled, giving some order to their random
placement. A cornice band under the eaves is punctuated
by tall, polychromed brackets.

The six exterior doorways of the house are protected by
roofed gates, each with a variation on the crazy quilt sticks.
A long one tucks itself under the porte-cochere to shelter
visitors and then politely steps into the house at the front
door. Only one is attached, to allow for a second story
balcony on the north side.

The meandering exterior structures only hint at the
colliding spaces inside. Here, within the taut exterior
walls, formally shaped rooms are placed in balanced
chaos, like shaken blocks in a toy box. The cylindrical,
elliptical, cubical, and rectangular volumes are
comfortable—functional, familiar, and easy to live with.
But their union is full of tension, offering extraordinary
spatial changes while moving between them and a new
vista at each doorway.

This house revels in eccentricity, but with precedent:
the Gothic revival of nearby houses; American craftsman
idiosyncrasy; or the rambling, connected farm buildings
of New England. The house melds old and new, packing
the traditional vernacular with a jumble of modern
volumetric surprises and new spatial relationships. These
and the constantly shifting light and views of the interior
and landscape keep this house good humored.

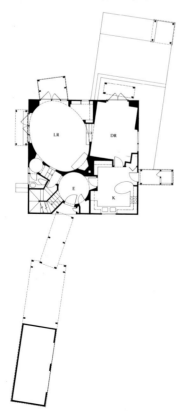

OPPOSITE TOP: North elevation, as it faces Long Island Sound.
Photo: Timothy Hursley

OPPOSITE BOTTOM: Stickwork gable is perceived from dining room.
Photo: Timothy Hursley

ABOVE: South-facing entry court features "drunken sailor" fence.
Photo: Timothy Hursley

LEFT: Detail of porte-cochere which greets visitors.
Photo: Timothy Hursley

Striar Jewish Community Center

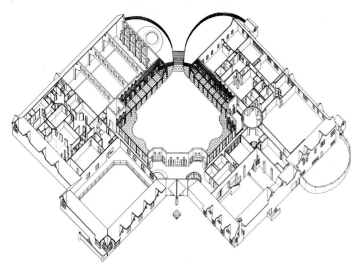

This building, sited on 16 wooded acres, consists of two long wings defining a courtyard. One, designated as the athletic wing, contains a gymnasium and indoor running track, a 25-meter pool, health clubs, dancing and exercise rooms. The other wing, a multifunctional element designated as the community wing, houses an auditorium, a library/gallery, nursery/day care for 160 children, teen and adult lounges, crafts areas, meeting rooms, a cafe, and offices.

Boston's South Area Jewish population helped design its new home. A cross-section of the entire community was encouraged to meet with Centerbrook to express views and preferences for the facility. The synagogue community was consulted as to its concerns. Centerbrook organized a week-long series of intensive design workshops in which 50 people from the South Area collaborated with the architects to design the community center. Groups accompanied the architects on site walks and were asked to envision their ideal natural environment—even tying yellow ribbons around their favorite trees.

Two stylistic vocabularies define the two-story building. The front facade, which faces away from the courtyard, is clad in shingles and lined with dormers to reflect the New England architecture of surrounding buildings. The courtyard, faced with Jerusalem limestone, stucco parapets, and wrought-iron trellises to suggest the most important and inspirational place on earth for Jews, communicates a sense of the Jewish culture assimilated within the larger culture of New England. The stone, stucco, and wrought iron are used throughout the holy city. The stone was quarried, cut, and hand-chiseled in Israel under the architect's direction, while interior mosaics designed by the architect were made by a Kibbutz in northern Israel.

OPPOSITE: Wrought-iron
trellis provides an armature
for vines.
Photo: Nick Wheeler

LEFT: Lavatory is filled with
bright color and pattern.
Photo: Steve Rosenthal

BELOW: Pool is surrounded
with unfinished concrete
structure.
Photo: Steve Rosenthal

Longmeadows House

ABOVE: Entry foyer frames
meadow views to south.
Photo: Mick Hales

OPPOSITE: Entry is through
north-facing porch.
Photo: Mick Hales

Longmeadows is a 15-lot subdivision located on a
hilltop. The property includes an open meadow of 15
acres surrounded by deciduous woodlands. This
high, open meadow is an exceptional place, and the
land planning enhances its qualities. The meadow
has been kept largely open, assuring long,
uninterrupted views out from the houses in the
surrounding woods. The trees give each house
privacy, but because most houses enjoy views over
the shared meadow, each house gives the impression
of being situated on an expansive piece of land.

The design of the houses celebrates the qualities of
the land—they, too, are expansive in feeling, with
steep roofs, tall chimneys, broad porches. Wood
shingles and painted trim evoke the feeling of turn-
of-the-century houses in Watch Hill, Newport, and
Bar Harbor. Stone walls and stout columns convey a
sense of stability and permanence. Paved courtyards
and landscaped terraces bring the visitor to brightly-
lit entrances, from which open spacious entry and
stair halls. Light enters from high windows, filtered
through many-paned windows as through the high
branches of the trees around the houses.

Within, rooms are generously proportioned.
Views open through tall windows, yet a sense of snug
enclosure is retained. Second floor verandahs provide
vantage points for surveying the landscape. Large
fireplaces reinforce the feeling of shelter. Materials
everywhere convey quality: oak floors, stone
fireplaces, wood cabinetwork and paneling.

ABOVE: House surmounts landscape with views over common meadow.
Photo: Mick Hales

LEFT: Entry motor court is bound by stone walls.
Photo: Mick Hales

OPPOSITE: View from living room through foyer to dining room.
Photo: Mick Hales

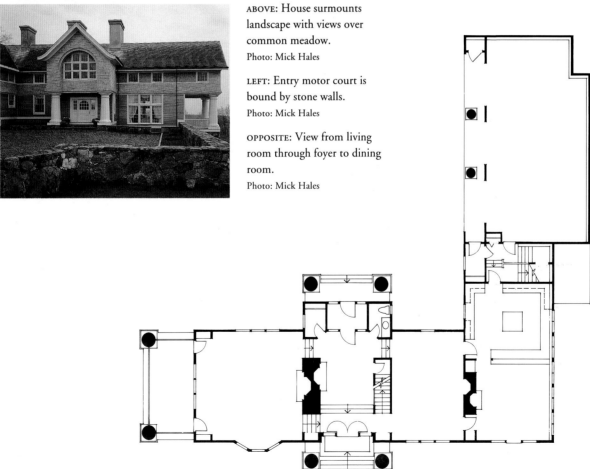

$\mathcal{W}$riston Art Center

Lawrence University
Appleton, Wisconsin

This art center fulfills a longstanding ambition at the university to make the fine arts an integral part of its campus life. The building had to relate to a six-story library to the north, a busy street to the east, the one-story student union to the south, and the campus green to the west. A week-long design workshop involving faculty, students, administrators, and friends of the university helped to clarify the expectations of the community to be served by the building.

The art center is designed as a campus landmark. The building is sited at the crossroads of the three main campus paths, and is virtually transparent so that passersby can peer into the galleries and the lower level studios with the ease and delight of a window shopper. Its materials and colors set it apart from other campus buildings built of various beige-colored stone, clapboard, and common brick, and bring a visual warmth to the long gray Wisconsin winters. It is the lowest building on campus, which allows glass towers to be seen under the canopy of trees of the campus green and to mark the place of the galleries, lecture hall, entry, and two loading docks which serve as symbols of the building's two main functions: One dock, Porta d'a Materia Prima, is for the delivery of raw materials to the studios, symbolizing the making of art. The other, Porta d'Arte, is for the delivery of art work to the galleries, symbolizing the study of art. The building's low height solved as well the formal problem of sitting between a high-rise library and a 20-foot-high student union by making the building, in effect, a low garden wall connecting the two. The art center is a sociable building, meant to attract people from all academic disciplines to the offerings within its garden walls.

ABOVE: Scale of art center is in keeping with residential neighborhood.
Photo: Paul Warchol

OPPOSITE: Entry is marked by exuberant color and ornament.
Photo: Paul Warchol

ABOVE: views into studios are gained from sidewalk level.
Photo: Paul Warchol

RIGHT: Galleries becoming increasingly smaller in scale.
Photo: Paul Warchol

OPPOSITE: Second floor circulation spine has views into courtyard.
Photo: Paul Warchol

ABOVE: Studios are
double-height and light
filled.
Photo: Paul Warchol

RIGHT: entry from plaza
is into a double-height
lobby.
Photo: Paul Warchol

OPPOSITE: Building's plaza
creates a gateway for campus
foot traffic.
Photo: Paul Warchol

BELOW: Art center has a low,
variegated profile.
Photo: Paul Warchol

SITE PLAN

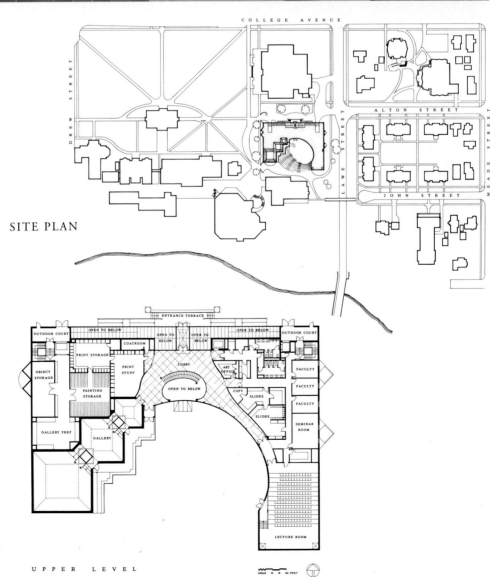

UPPER LEVEL

$\mathcal{R}$oss-Lacy House

This house of 1,400 square feet serves as the main house and entry gate to an estate of large trees, rolling lawns, and carefully gardened outcroppings. Approached from downhill it is at first apparently symmetrical. On closer inspection, its five parts—a dining room/living room wing, a bedroom/study wing, a central vestibule, and two chimneys—declare their gentle independence. While the house is generally at rest, it is also animated like its pastoral setting.

The two pavilions are set at slightly different angles to the center, and the chimneys are of different sizes and angles. The pavilions bend around the center to create an entry court downhill while also separating to announce uphill vistas.

Inside, the movement of parts becomes all the more apparent. The organization offers dramatic surprises of light and views to those moving through the house, while still allowing the decorum of rooms for human activity.

Exterior materials are simple: vertical cedar siding, trimless at doors to give a sense of depth to the walls, stops at a horizontal band reminiscent of older local houses. A lead-coated copper roof is durable and beautiful, reflecting the sky's changing color from morning to night and from season to season.

Details are spare but careful, from wide-board pine flooring to simple Greek Revival trim around doors and windows. The fireplaces extend from the base of their freestanding chimneys into the house as temple forms, with hand colored cementitious plaster and playful brick patterns under paint.

With its high, airy spaces, twelve French doors, and large windows, this house is gracious and welcoming. Like the words on the Petit Trianon (Marie Antionette's famous home), "Parve sed optima," it is "Small but enough."

ABOVE: Corridor from entry with view toward bedroom.
Photo: Timothy Hursley

OPPOSITE: Pristine house forms surmount the landscape.
Photo: Timothy Hursley

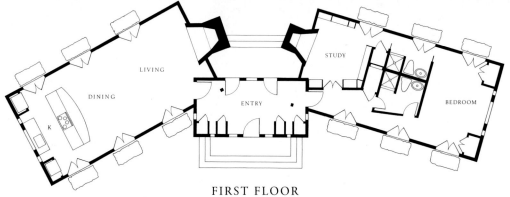

FIRST FLOOR

OPPOSITE CLOCKWISE FROM
TOP: Living room forms and
furniture reflect simple
detailing.
Photo: Timothy Hursley

House nestles into its
hillside site.
Photo: Timothy Hursley

Exterior detailing is inspired by
Greek Revival architecture.
Photo: Timothy Hursley

ABOVE: Entry hall allows access
to house's private and public
realms.
Photo: Timothy Hursley

*H*arper House Porch

This porch, built to replace an open deck, adds nearly 50 percent to the living-dining-kitchen spaces of a small contemporary house. The double-square plan allows one half of the porch to be a sitting space, adjacent to the living room. The other half of the porch is a dining space, opening off the kitchen. Doors at both ends of the porch open to the yard and woods.

The porch's cedar trim and sloping ceiling match the siding and ceilings of the main house, and the colors in the furniture echo the house's trim color. The high gable allows for air circulation and opens views up to the tree-tops. The large trellis elements in the screens frame and enhance views and give at once feelings of openness and enclosure.

LEFT: Interior is distinguished by carefully detailed natural materials.
Photo: Timothy Hursley

OPPOSITE: Porch extends south from main house.
Photo: Timothy Hursley

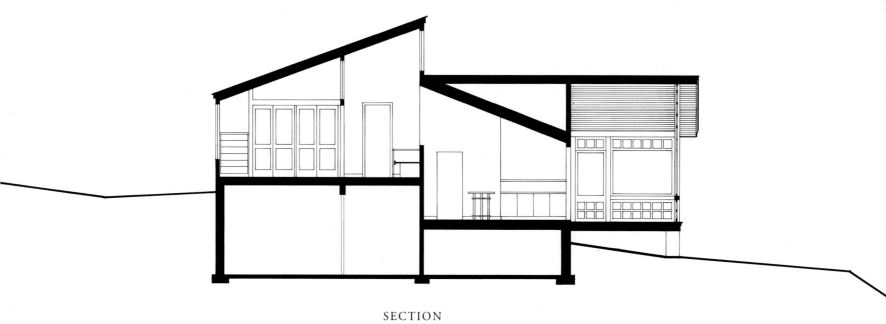

SECTION

House on the Connecticut Shore

ABOVE: Interior is
distinguished by integral
shutters that modulate light.
Photo: Mick Hales

OPPOSITE: House as it
overlooks Long Island Sound.
Photo: Mick Hales

This house occupies a three-acre site with a southerly
view of Long Island Sound. To the southeast is the
lee side of a rocky island, to the southwest a view to
the Thimble Islands, a rocky archipelago reminiscent
of the Maine coast.

The house sits atop an historic quarry, filled in
long ago, from which granite for the base of the
Statue of Liberty was obtained. Vegetation around
the site's edges are hemlock, cedar, and black pines.
A previous owner of the land had built a seawall of
large granite boulders and a boat ramp.

Because of its location in a flood zone, the house's
first habitable floor had to be at a minimum
elevation of 16 feet. All nonstructural elements below
that elevation had to be made to break away, and
structural elements had to withstand severe storms.

The program called for a year-round house of
7,500 square feet, including outdoor decks and
terraces. It was the owners' request that the house be
large enough to accommodate house guests
comfortably and that it be oriented as directly as
possible to the water.

The organizing concept of the house is a
collection of pavilions which frame views from each
of the house's principal spaces. The living room
enjoys a view of the sound; the dining room looks
southwest toward the Thimble Islands and summer
sunsets; the study looks partly to the water and partly
at the end of a rocky island; the master bedroom
looks at the quiet lee side of a nearby island. The
house is configured on the site in a way that has the
visitor entering the automobile courtyard without
yet having seen the water. It is not until the stairs
have been mounted and the house entered that the
visitor sees through the hall, across the angled living
room, and down the boat ramp to the water.

ABOVE: South-facing windows frame multiple views.
Photo: Mick Hales

RIGHT: Poolhouse and pool area is screened with lattice.
Photo: Mick Hales

OPPOSITE: Native granite walls bound the house from the water.
Photo: Mick Hales

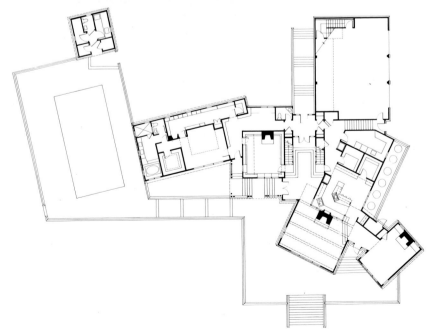

*E*ast Lyme Library and Community Center

Modern despite its classicism, this 35,000-square-foot building combines a public town library with senior and youth centers, offices for a visiting nurse association, the town parks and recreation department, and a multi-purpose meeting room. The town requested that each of these maintain a separate identity while being housed in a single story building with New England character. The site complicated these requirements. It borders residences, wetlands, and the Smith Harris House, an historic Greek Revival farmstead on the National Register.

Studies revealed just enough room to fit the building and required parking on the narrow site. The building is located on the north half of the site, allowing the south end to serve as an entry and parking "orchard," sunny in winter and shady in summer. The tripartite building has three open pavilion entries. The longest of these, in the middle, leads to a high lobby in which all departments have indoor entries. The youth and senior centers claim the two other pavilions as their own outdoor entries.

The sloping roofs required by the client are massive. Their scale is broken down with Greek Revival pavilions and dormers reflecting the Smith Harris House. A gallery pavilion, almost the same size as the house, juts out the back of the lobby to face it. Trim and fenestration throughout the building, though newly invented, recalls the house's style along columnar brick piers and pediments of the three building wings.

The building's space is often free-form, its rhythms are jazzy, and finishes are modern throughout. It thus combines the familiar and the unexpected to reassure on the one hand, and entice and stimulate on the other.

ABOVE: Gabled porches establish entry to building's various functions.
Photo: Norman McGrath

RIGHT: Main lobby gives building a civic scale.
Photo: Norman McGrath

OPPOSITE: Library features comfortable reading room with pendant lights.
Photo: Norman McGrath

Conklin House

ABOVE: Tent-like fabric
creates soft edge in living
room and is in keeping with
room's pavilion arrangement.
Photo: Norman McGrath

OPPOSITE: Addition appears
as a pavilion separate from
the main house.
Photo: Norman McGrath

This house stands on an acre lot near New York City, and though neighboring house are quite close, the wedge shape of the lot (narrow at the street, wide at the back) together with mature plantings on every side, give the house a remarkable degree of privacy. The planning of the original house, however, took little advantage of the property's seclusion. The clients, a couple with grown children, wished to change the house in which they had lived for 20 years to meet present and future needs.

The original 1930s "Art Deco French Provincial" style building has a center hall plan, enlivened by the main stair, which curves around in a generous arc, breaking through the orthogonal enclosure of the house. A tall, curving, glass block window floods both stories of the hall with light. The clients wanted an addition that would take better advantage of the site and would provide a second living room on the first floor, convertible into a master suite. The clients also observed that since the yard sloped up toward the southeast (its widest side) the addition might fit best at an angle to the southwest, enclosing the space of the yard and affording the longest possible view, yet this seemed at odds with the existing plan.

The solution lay in the house's style and its glass-block stairway. A new octagonal tower would act as a hinge between the house and the addition. The new room, almost a separate addition, is rotated into the best position to take full advantage of the site. The new living room is a pavilion inside as well as out, with windows on all four sides and a tent-like canopy that hangs from the ceiling and filters light from clerestory windows. A new bathroom housed in a smaller pavilion rotates farther (using a small dressing room as a hinge) to complete the enclosure of the yard.

LEFT: Entry foyer links addition to original house.
Photo: Norman McGrath

BELOW: View of living room looking back toward foyer.
Photo: Norman McGrath

OPPOSITE, TOP: Addition's discrete elements are akin to original house forms.
Photo: Norman McGrath

OPPOSITE, BOTTOM: Front of original house blends with addition to right.
Photo: Norman McGrath

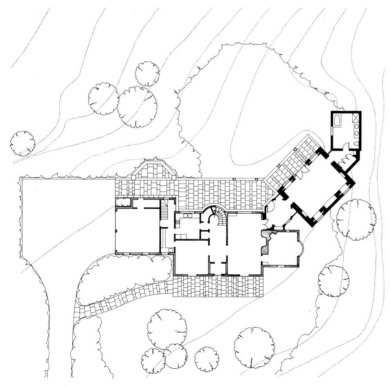

SITE AND FIRST FLOOR

*P*ershing Point Plaza

ABOVE: Banding of
rejuvenated lobby relates to
exterior.
Photo: Rion Rizzo/Creative Sources

OPPOSITE FROM TOP: New entry
is defined by metal trellis.
Photo: Rion Rizzo/Creative Sources

Three building blocks before
renovation.

Renovated blocks sport added
elements that tie them together.
Photo: Rion Rizzo/Creative Sources

Entry trellis is slowly covered
with vegetation.
Photo: Rion Rizzo/Creative Sources

Pershing Point Plaza attempts to bring architectural
distinction to a complex of three banal 1950s office
buildings by removing incongruous elements from
their facades and introducing details evocative of the
buildings' Modernist roots. The unusual blue color
of the facades was also a challenge. For all this color's
vibrance, it seemed to merge with the sky without
the impact one might have expected.

A two-dimensional grid was found to underlie the
three facades. It allowed introduction of a number of
horizontal metal bands of varying widths. Colored a
very dark shade of blue, these bands, as the principal
new Modernist detail, weave the three buildings
together into a unit and introduce horizontality to
an otherwise vertical composition. New windows
and wall tiles in dark blue have also been added.
Together, these elements interact with the existing
blue brick to brighten up the facades and to
introduce a much-needed two dimensional
complexity to the composition.

A new brise soleil was designed for the wall over
the entry—a massive concrete porte cochere was
replaced with a new steel canopy, and a double row
of oak trees now shades a sidewalk dining terrace
that is popular in the mild Atlanta climate. At the
four corners of a pedestrian bridge—and at other key
points of entry—a new infrastructure of lighting
stanchions helps evoke Pershing Point's Modernist
persona. Inside, the buildings' two separate existing
circulation systems are joined into a single new lobby
with the same banding motif as the exterior.

Noteworthy to this project is its revisionist
method of introducing Modernist detail to a dowdy
office building that, like so many others in the
commercial environment, previously lacked a full
expression of its Bauhaus heritage.

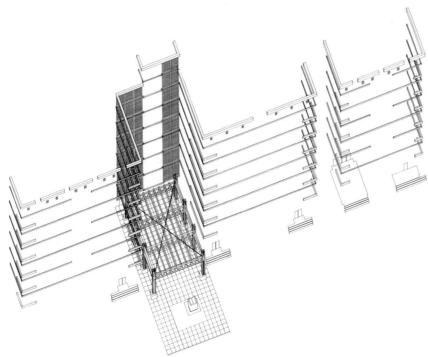

$\mathcal{A}$ugusciak House

The site of this weekend house, a knoll close by a freshwater pond, offers handsome views in every direction. To the west is the pond, screened from the house by a stand of deciduous trees. To the north are deciduous woods and rolling topography. Evergreen trees to the east provide year-round privacy from the approach road and driveway. To the south the knoll opens out onto a long meadow. The drive approaching the site descends a long hill, crosses a stream, and climbs a short way to the house.

A large, simply-shaped house would overwhelm the delicate character of the existing knoll and trees. It seemed, rather, that a house that appeared to be an aggregate of smaller pieces would be more in keeping with the landscape.

The house's design evolved with the pieces of the building wrapped around an entry car court. The house screens the cars from view from most outdoor living spaces, and the continuous eave draws the different elements of the building into a unified whole. Covered porches on the pond and entry sides of the house extend the living spaces out into the landscape. The chimney masses mark places where the geometry of the building shifts. Inside, the stair to the second floor bedrooms passes into a chimney mass, climbs through it, and emerges on an opposite side at the higher level, allowing those more private spaces to seem to be at a still further remove from the rest of the house.

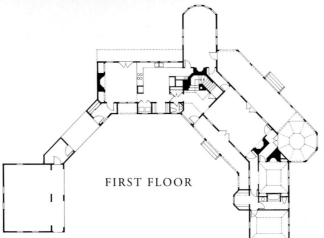

FIRST FLOOR

ABOVE: Northwest side of house is dominated by porch with views toward water.
Photo: Robert L. Harper

RIGHT: Stair passage is carved out of chimney mass.
Photo: Robert L. Harper

OPPOSITE: Massive chimneys visually anchor house to the site.
Photo: Robert L. Harper

*H*ouse in Connecticut

This project balances the natural and the man-made
components of a large estate by manipulating the
landscape, adding a few generous spaces to an existing
farmhouse, and transforming a nearby fire-damaged
poolhouse into a special "folly."

The main structure, an old farmhouse that had been
added to many times in typical New England fashion,
lay at the end of a long drive. Additions to it were
opposite the approach side, which offers a broad view of
a handsome meadow and forest set ablaze on summer
nights by spectacular sunsets. A large living room was
added to the house, with a long curving wall of windows
facing west. Designed for enjoying sunsets and for
entertaining, the room's 68-foot length is modulated by
an hour-glass shape that varies in width from 12 to 22
feet, creating spaces for small and large gatherings.

Just north of the main house stands a small
poolhouse structure that had been partially destroyed
by fire and subsequently repaired. This modest
building was in full view of the main house's new
living room, so its transformation into something
worthy became urgent. The rejuvenated poolhouse
encloses the adjacent outdoor pool and adds a covered
seating area and small kitchen.

A dual orientation of the poolhouse toward the main
house and the entry drive provides the living room with
an interesting focus and the drive with a terminus. The
covered seating takes the form of a gazebo that faces the
house, with the poolhouse's roof rising up gradually to
cover it. A new facade, three feet from the building's
face, is composed of a lattice screen that extends across
the poolhouse's old windows and door, allowing them
to remain unchanged. At the facade's center, an entry
dormer and chimney lock the building squarely onto
the axis of the drive—providing a satisfying new focus
to the drive's extraordinary alley of trees.

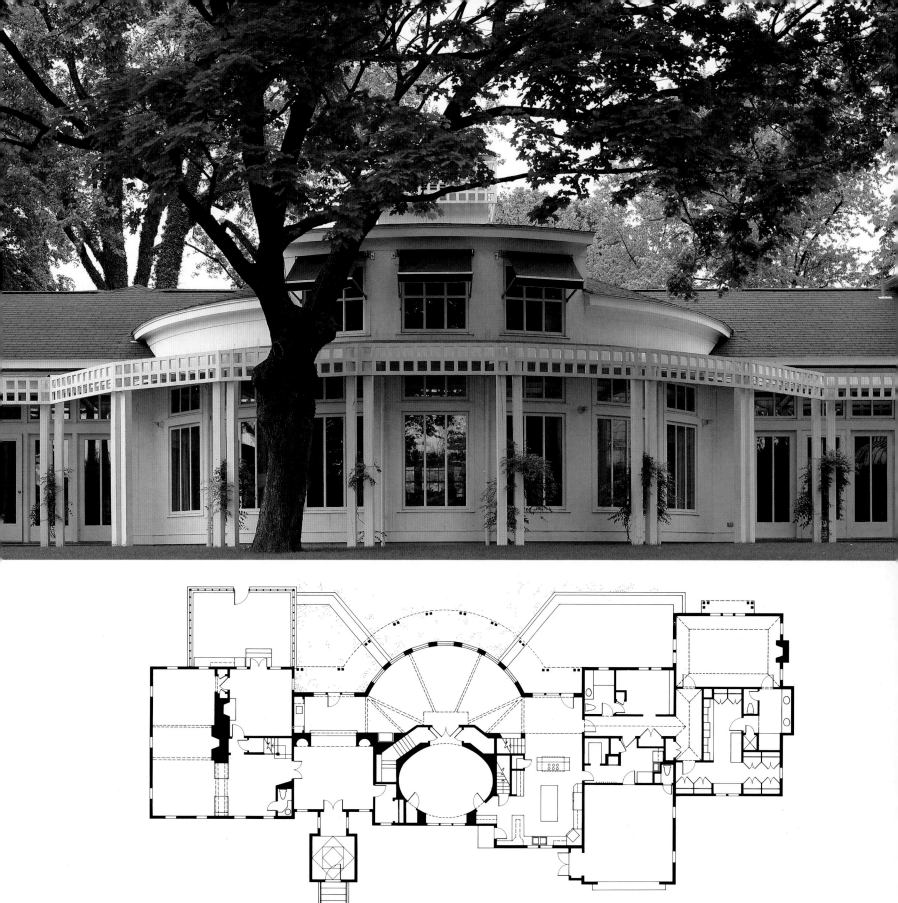

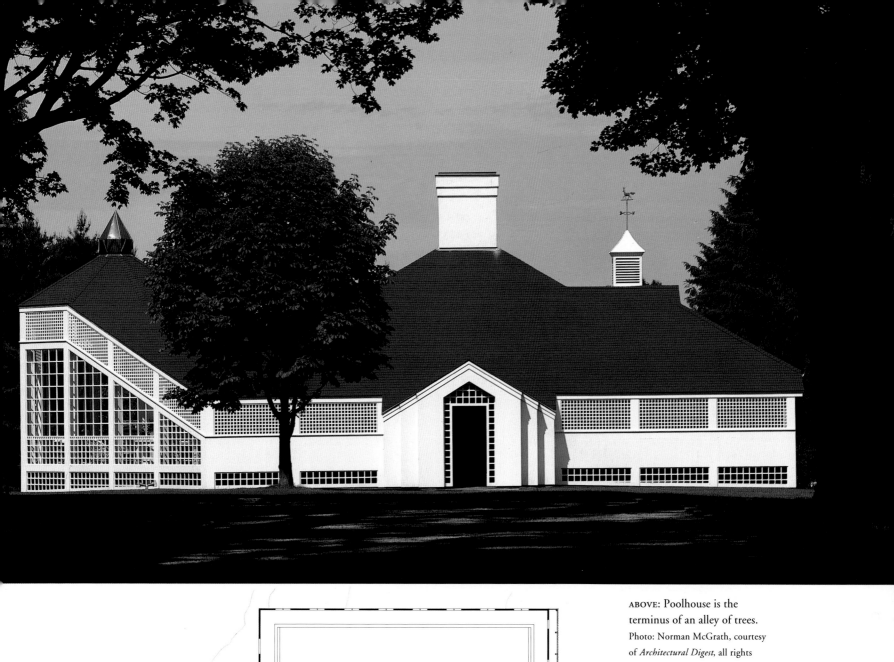

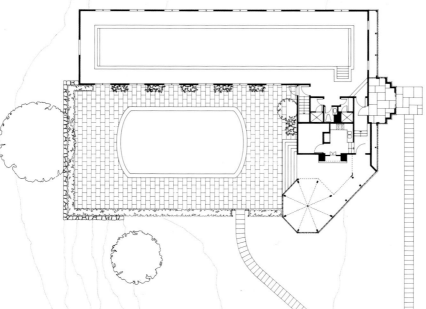

*W*oodlands Cabin

A simple rectangle in plan, the central space of this rustic cabin is formed by its traditional log structure. The building sits on piles to avoid disturbance of the flood plain at the edge of a loblolly pine forest.

It is a place for quiet contemplation, with views across vast marshland to the south.

At the entry to the cabin, split log steps lead up to treetrunk columns which support the roof beams. These are spaced irregularly to mimic the surrounding pines. At the rear of the cabin, the sitting deck just outside three large French doors has a faux truss overhead, like a tangle of forest branches. Inside, the main sitting space is octagonal. Its fireplace is framed by tree trunks and roots, and is topped by a copper-clad chimney chase. Tucked behind this is a short entry hall and bathroom.

Closed in and protected by woods at the entry side, and glassy at the rear for the view, this cabin provides a safe haven in the midst of the wilderness to enjoy the wonders of nature.

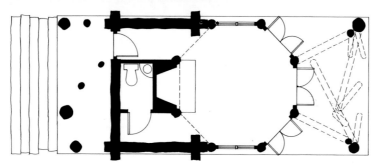

PAVILLION

THIS PAGE: The cabin is at home in its wilderness site.
Photo: Norman McGrath

OPPOSITE: Rustic interior is distinguished with copper-clad fireplace.
Photo: Norman McGrath.

$\mathcal{R}$eid House II

TOP: "Bow House" offers sunset views and curving bench.
Photo: Timothy Hursley

ABOVE: Rooftop deck is ship-like in its atmosphere.
Photo: Timothy Hursley

Located on the south shore of Cape Cod, this summer house was designed for a couple whose permanent home in Ohio is also a Centerbrook creation. The request from the client was for a house that would take in not only the westward panorama of beach, ocean, and sunset, but also rise above the tree-tops to gain views to the east of a small, boat-filled harbor while keeping within the scale of nearby houses. In fact, a neighborhood review committee had to be satisfied that the house's design was sympathetic to neighboring turn-of-the-century shingle-style residences. The house was to accommodate more than a dozen relatives (including small children), and the client's desire for a playful vacation house with the aura of a seaside retreat. It also had to be substantial enough to withstand a hundred-year flood (which it did, twice, in the summer and fall of 1991).

The house was envisioned as a fantastic ship, with berths inside and decks outside. The screened Bow House takes its place at the prow, backed by two pavilions devoted to entertainment and relaxation, respectively. Below the raised first floor, an open space spreads out amongst the underpinnings of the house. Ballasted with mounds of sand and large boulders, this belly of the "ship" is a place of exploration for the children.

The first floor, devoted to living spaces and a master bedroom suite, is distinguished in its open interior, the focus of which is a magical sitting room and fireplace decorated with seashells. The room's shallow domed ceiling swirls with celestial bodies, while fantastic fish dive over the mantel, all painted by the architect. The second floor contains guest quarters and a skylit living room with sweeping views of the ocean and harbor.

ABOVE: The house stretches
across the site as a large ship.
Photo: Timothy Hursley

RIGHT: As it faces the ocean,
the house opens to views.
Photo: Timothy Hursley

ABOVE Second floor living
room has expansive views of
the waterfront.
Photo: Timothy Hursley

RIGHT: First floor sitting
room fireplace sports shells
pressed into wet concrete.
Photo: Timothy Hursley

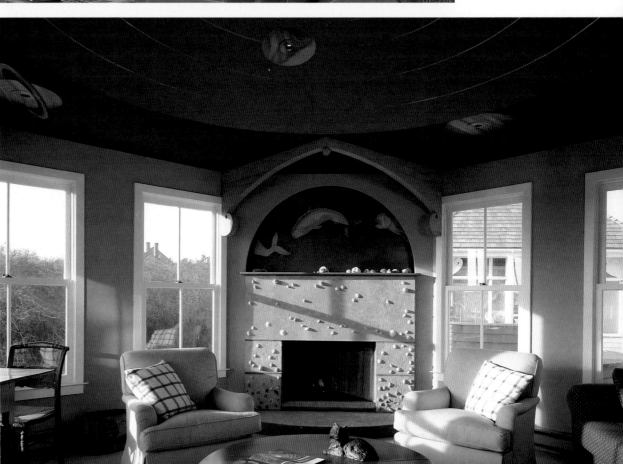

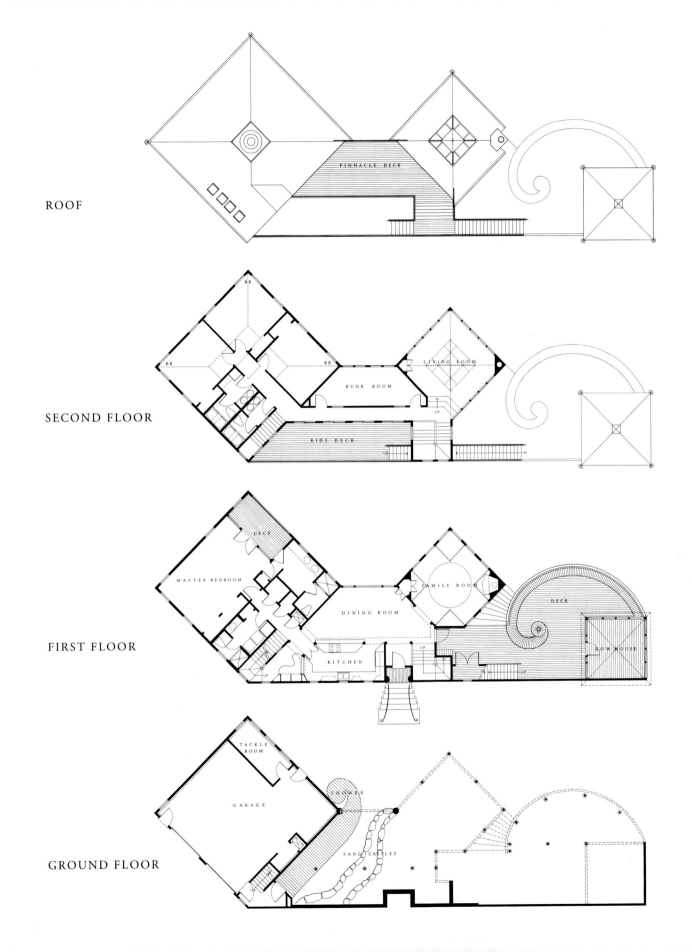

ROOF

SECOND FLOOR

FIRST FLOOR

GROUND FLOOR

*H*enderson Hall Computer Resources Center

SECOND FLOOR

FIRST FLOOR

OPPOSITE: North elevation is punctuated by small square windows of interior stair.
Photo: Norman McGrath

The program for Henderson Hall called for a new computer resources center at Bard College—a small liberal arts institution in Duchess County, New York. It was to contain a teaching classroom, the gift of IBM; a drop-in facility which students might use day and night; and various offices and storage spaces. Capital and life cycle costs were to be minimal, and the design was to be simple enough that the college's in-house building and grounds crew could construct it with little outside assistance.

An existing small computer center located in a one-story structure over a central boiler bunker was found to be the ideal location for the new facility, so a plan was developed that called for demolition of the existing one-story structure but retention of the bunker as a base for the new building.

A three-story structure was developed atop the base, with the IBM classroom on the first floor, the drop-in facility on the second, and offices and storage on the third. The new structure was allowed to overhang the base on all sides, with a stair on the north elevation expressed as a major element. Trees mask the building's other three sides.

The Bard campus derives its character from the estate architecture of rural Duchess County. Henderson Hall was developed in that spirit, to be somewhat reminiscent of a barn or estate outbuilding—an effect heightened by the farm ventilator on its ridge and its rustic brackets.

For ease of maintenance and low capital cost, the college requested vinyl siding and inexpensive windows. The building's base is painted a dark, cool gray to contrast with the warm color of the siding.

The completed Henderson Hall animates the south side of a heretofore unresolved central courtyard with a structure that is vertical enough and has a persona strong enough to hold its own against the five- and six-story stone residential halls that surround it.

$\mathcal{P}$ond House

ABOVE: Pool area is defined
by changing rooms, screened
porch, guest house, and
trellis fence.
Photo: Jeff Goldberg/Esto

OPPOSITE: Domed entry
hall is warmed with honey-
colored plaster walls and
wood molding.
Photo: Jeff Goldberg/Esto

This summer house for a family of six is a village-like
complex of pavilions sitting on a small peninsula
between a long freshwater pond and marsh. Its
15,000 square feet are spread out to keep the scale
intimate, roofs low, and the buildings nestled into a
scrub oak forest.

The house is an amalgam of New England
architecture. Curved roofs and dormers recall
Nantucket shipwrights' houses. Vertical battening
and stickwork that holds large overhanging eaves are
reminiscent of Victorian cottages on Martha's
Vineyard. The arched windows, which step up and
down within the battening, are at once Gothic and
Modern. Stone walls on the site and main house are
in the New England tradition, laid in monumental
bands. Inside, painted narrow boards are used to
lend a gentle texture to the living room ceiling and
the walls of the dining room, guest living rooms, and
master bedroom suite. Colored plaster warms the
domed entry hall.

The buildings are arranged in two offset arcs
enclosing a welcoming auto court. In the center is a
tower, open below as an entry porch to the main
house and enclosed above as a glassy study for one of
the clients, a professor. Behind this the main house is
three attached pavilions, stitched together by two
long hallways. Across the court from the main house
are two guest houses connected at their entries with a
breezeway, which faces an outdoor pool protected
from the driveway court by a zig-zag trellis fence.

The site was kept as natural as possible, while still
leaving space for outdoor play. Except for the lawn,
drive, and court, the landscape surrounding the
house was restored with low-bush blueberry and
other native plants between the oak trees.

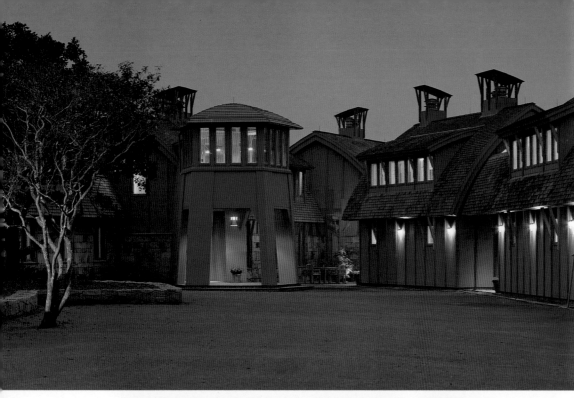

OPPOSITE LEFT: Pool area is framed by screened porch and guest house.
Photo: Jeff Goldberg/Esto

OPPOSITE RIGHT: Stepped fence is surmounted with curved trellis.
Photo: Jeff Goldberg/Esto

TOP: A tower with a private study at its top is the focal point of the entry court.
Photo: Jeff Goldberg/Esto

ABOVE: Living room features a welcoming granite fireplace.
Photo: Jeff Goldberg/Esto

RIGHT: Rising sun enlivens exterior stone walls and colorful brackets.
Photo: Jeff Goldberg/Esto

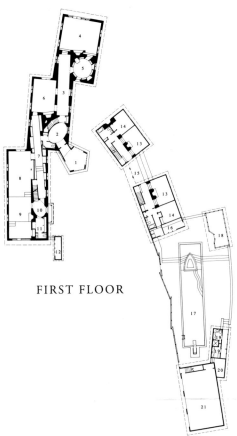

FIRST FLOOR

$\mathcal{M}$itchell-Haney House

ABOVE: House's new profile
surmounts entry drive.
Photo: Timothy Hursley

OPPOSITE: Third-floor
interior is distinguished by
new twisting chimney.
Photo: Timothy Hursley

Originally a small, square, two-story box of a building with a shallow hip roof, this turn-of-the-century house had been enlarged by previous owners to provide pleasant first-floor living spaces. The tiny bedrooms and bath on the second floor, however, were inadequate for a young family requiring space for a growing child and a home office.

The house is situated close to the property boundaries and lateral expansion in any direction would require zoning variances or compromise the existing first-floor living spaces. The logical direction for growth, therefore, was upwards. There was little headroom under the existing roof, but a new, steeper roof could provide a master bedroom suite and bath, leaving the second floor free for children and office.

Previous additions, wrapped around the original box at the first floor, had given the house a layered, "wedding cake" profile. The new roof develops this idea further, keeping the hipped corners low and placing a room-sized gabled dormer on each face of the house. A cupola as a top layer offers views of the Connecticut River. New cedar clapboard siding is used for the exterior, while the roofs and decorative sidewall elements are clad in cedar shingles.

The gables provide four new rooms around the existing central stair: bedroom, sitting room (placed to take advantage of the view), dressing room, and bath. The bath is the only new room that is enclosed for privacy; each of the others opens into neighboring rooms to borrow space. The cupola is turned 45 degrees to the main house in order to afford larger windows, which extend down into the valleys between the dormers. The new chimney twists and offsets in a startling way as it passes through the third-story spaces in order to leave the cupola free for use.

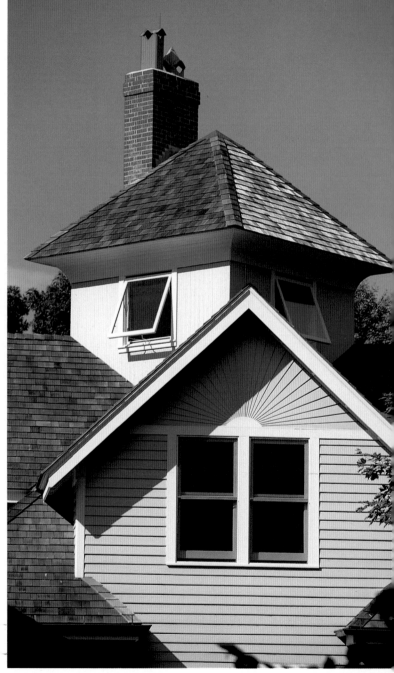

ABOVE: Third floor spaces
are open to each other
around chimney.
Photo: Timothy Hursley

RIGHT: Details include
clapboard fan in gable and
decorative chimney pots.
Photo: Robert L. Harper

OPPOSITE, LEFT: House
before third-story addition.
Photo: Robert L. Harper

OPPOSITE, RIGHT: Third
story and cupola complete
"wedding cake" profile.
Photo: Timothy Hursley

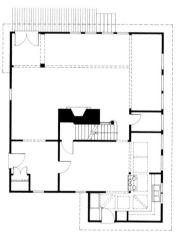

FIRST FLOOR

SECOND FLOOR

THIRD FLOOR

CUPOLA

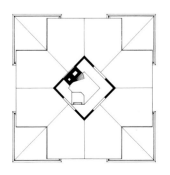

Killingworth House

ABOVE: Original white house's additions blend with landscape to diminish scale.
Photo: Jeff Goldberg/Esto

LEFT: Sitting area windows are voids in the trusswork.
Photo: Jeff Goldberg/Esto

OPPOSITE: Truss at entry is repeated in foyer.
Photo: Jeff Goldberg/Esto

A small white farmhouse on a tree-lined country road had been in the client's family for many years as a weekend retreat. Its interior consisted of many small and rather dark rooms. The owners wished to double the size of the house to include a new large living room for entertaining, a new master bedroom wing, and a new kitchen and sunroom. Two tiny second floor bedrooms were combined into one. But the clients didn't want the house to look big—or out of place—on the narrow road.

The small scale of the complex is maintained by making the additions a group of barn-like buildings in colors different from the original house. The master bedroom and porte-cochere at the family entrance are simple, gable-roofed structures, painted barn red. The new living room is another barn-like box painted slate gray to blend into the shadows under huge maple trees that surround the house. This wing is located behind the bedroom wing to reduce the apparent size of this large element from the road. The original house remains white, as the focal point of the composition.

Light is brought in high through the gable ends of the rooms. The window shapes recall both the structural system of barns and the branches of the large maple trees. The south wall of the living room is illuminated by two skylights at the ridge and by nine small windows that admit shafts of winter sunlight. The ceiling in the living room and bedroom are white "waney edged" boards from a local mill, traditionally used for the sheathing of barns, backed up by plywood sheathing painted bright blue. The high roof is supported by wood trusses like those used in Connecticut mills.

ABOVE: Living room is flooded with illumination from skylights and square windows.
Photo: Jeff Goldberg/Esto

LEFT: "Waney edged" boards are used for ceilings, articulated with blue background.
Photo: Jeff Goldberg/Esto

OPPOSITE FROM TOP: Gray entry element is joined to porte-cochere.
Photo: Jeff Goldberg/Esto

Living room's window wall permits views north toward country road.
Photo: Jeff Goldberg/Esto

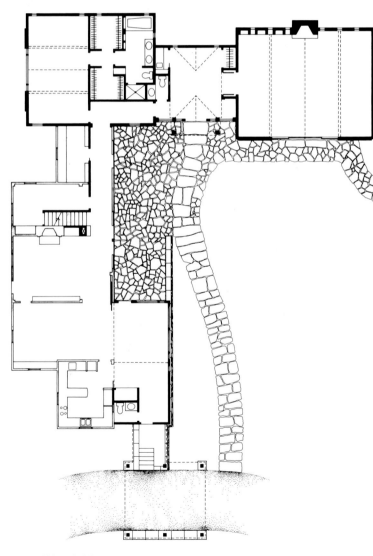

FIRST FLOOR

*H*ouse in the Country

ABOVE: Living room fireplace, ceiling, and trusses create an imagined medieval setting.
Photo: Jeff Goldberg/Esto

OPPOSITE: Bright red roofs contribute to rural esthetic.
Photo: Jeff Goldberg/Esto

This house is on a hilltop in rural Connecticut. Prior to its design, the clients cleared much of the land and uncovered many fine old stone walls. With the help of a local farmer, they returned the woods to the open fields that were typical of the area a century ago. In clearing the land, a spectacular view across a valley to a mountain was revealed.

The clients felt that the traditional rural character of the region, with its dairy farms, barns, and sheds, presented a context that should guide the house's architecture. To be accommodated within the house were the frequent piano recitals and a rare collection of German literature.

The house was designed somewhat in the local vernacular as a simple white barn with a red roof, but one that stands broadside to a square, graveled "barnyard." Entry into the yard is opposite the center of the house, through a farm gate hung from a pair of matched sheds.

The hillside into which the house is built has been shaped into a podium. Care was given to the precise view that would be framed by the living room window. As one approaches the house, the entry drive drops in elevation, allowing the house to be seen first against the backdrop of the distant mountain. As one proceeds, the mountain recedes, and upon arrival at the house, it is completely blocked from view. Once in the front hall, a large living room window reveals the mountain.

The living room, which is several steps down and on axis with the front door, is large enough for recitals with two grand pianos. The living room ceiling and an associated pair of substantial scissors trusses are painted in alternating bands of medieval red and green. A big stone fireplace is set into a niche that is marked overhead by an inverted, brightly painted pyramid.

LEFT: Entry hall is distinguished by high, light-filled space.
Photo: Jeff Goldberg/Esto

OPPOSITE, LEFT: Second floor library allows views across and into entry hall.
Photo: Jeff Goldberg/Esto

OPPOSITE, RIGHT: Exterior is inspired by nearby rural vernacular architecture.
Photo: Jeff Goldberg/Esto

OPPOSITE, BOTTOM: Fireplace has stripes of color and inverted pyramid motif.
Photo: Norman McGrath

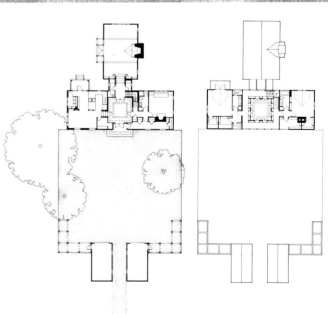

$\mathcal{M}$iller House

ABOVE: Exposed wood structure supports barn-like imagery.
Photo: Jeff Goldberg/Esto

OPPOSITE: From the west, house appears as a collection of farm buildings.
Photo: Jeff Goldberg/Esto

When viewed from a distance, this house at first appears to be a collection of farm buildings in a meadow: a large gable-roofed box, a small gable-roofed box, and a cylinder. Each is stained a different color to further emphasize their difference in form and size. The windows on the entry side are purposefully small to exaggerate the apparent size of the buildings, in effect making a small house appear to be the size of a barn.

Two tiny outbuildings are located approximately 200 feet from the house. A poolhouse tucked into the fold of a hillside is a diminutive, two-story gable-roofed box. At the brow of the hill is a two-seat gazebo constructed of lath, like a corn crib. Both structures are painted dark aubergine, the color of shadows in the woods, to make them disappear on the hillside. They are connected to the house by narrow boardwalks raised 18 inches above the ground, which provide dry walking surfaces just below the top of the meadow grass.

Because the house is sited back from the edge of a hill, there are strikingly different views from each floor level. On the ground floor, the view is across a hay field, which grows right up to the house. The grasses are high in the summer so the view of the Berkshire Mountains from the living room is through and across tall grass. The valley to the southeast becomes visible only from the second floor, from which more mountains are visible. The top of the silo is a sitting platform with a panoramic view of the entire property, and the mountains in the distance. Throughout the house are secret lofts, passageways, and tiny places in contrast to the big barn-like central space, which has an exposed mortise-and-tenon structure and is finished in white pine. Areas off the central space are painted white to provide a background for the colorful objects collected by the owners.

RIGHT: East elevation offers views over tall-grass meadows.
Photo: Jeff Goldberg/Esto

BELOW: Elevated boardwalk permits exploration of meadow and views beyond.
Photo: Jeff Goldberg/Esto

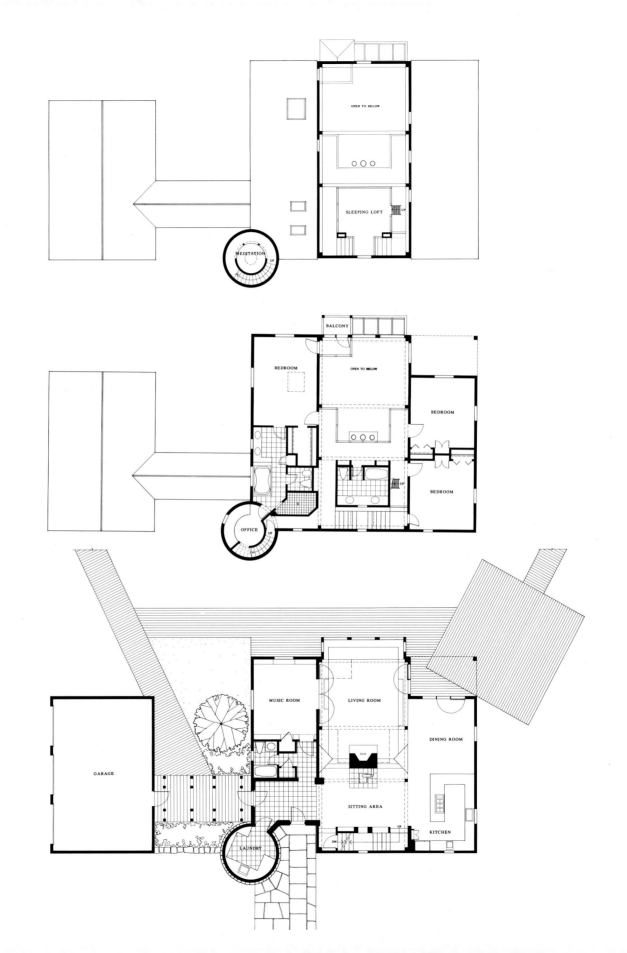

$\mathcal{M}$arsh Estate

ABOVE: Round dining room
is encircled with original
landscape watercolor murals.
Photo: Norman McGrath

OPPOSITE: At dusk the main
house is a luminous beacon
on the water.
Photo: Norman McGrath

Stretches of marshland and low-lying pine forests make up this 3,000-acre estate, which comprises two sets of buildings—one, close to the road, is a farm whose main purpose is to maintain and oversee wildlife habitats. The other, at the edges of the marsh, is a lodge which can sleep many visitors.

The lodge is built on pilings 10 feet above grade, and is divided into four parts—two wings, a central living room looking south to the marsh, and a central tower facing north to the sanctuary.

One enters up a "drunken" stair at the base of the tower to a circumnavigating deck, which is supported by tree trunk columns. From the tops of these columns sprout random branch-like brackets of dimensional lumber, which support the second floor balconies and roof overhang. To the right and left of the central stair are doors to the grand entry halls of each wing.

While at first glance this house may seem to be a reproduction of a turn-of-the-century wilderness lodge, it is both modern and playful—rooms inside are formed in clear volumes that are surprisingly jumbled within the outside walls. Spaces go from low to high and back again, with all the scale changes of Alice's Wonderland. Hidden doors and passageways surprise visitors at every turn. Natural tree work (co-designed with craftsman Daniel Mack), like that of classical Adirondack "great camps" is found in stair rails, balcony rails, and in the master bedroom suite.

Designed to commune with nature—sitting within her and echoing her as well—one moment the lodge appears as a large bird spreading its wings, the next as the marsh and forests that surround it.

ABOVE: Corridor outside
dining room leads to
kitchen and service spaces.
Photo: Norman McGrath

ABOVE RIGHT: Massive granite
fireplace in living room is
surrounded with stickwork.
Photo: Norman McGrath

RIGHT: Guest wing lounge is
a cathedral of branches,
reaching to natural light.
Photo: Norman McGrath

ABOVE: Stickwork detail at stairway railing.
Photo: Norman McGrath

ABOVE, RIGHT: Copper sink near dining room is an inventive watercourse.
Photo: Norman McGrath

BOTTOM: Entry to master bedroom wing has stepped fireplace.
Photo: Norman McGrath

ABOVE: Tower marks the main entries and offers sweeping wetlands views.
Photo: Norman McGrath

RIGHT: Promenade is guarded by tree-trunk columns lashed in rope.
Photo: Norman McGrath

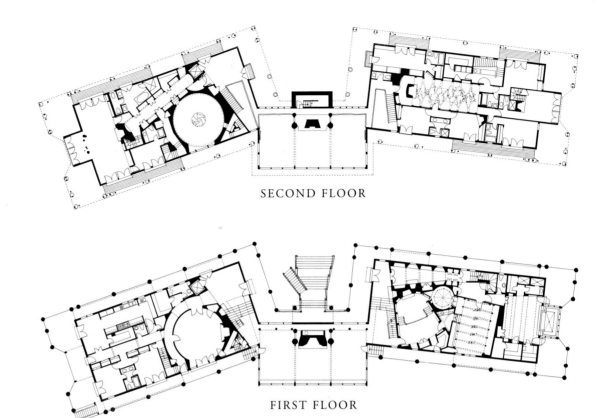

SECOND FLOOR

FIRST FLOOR

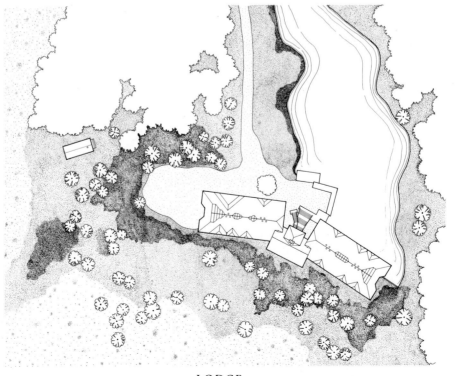

LODGE

$\mathcal{A}$FTERWORD

The partners of Centerbrook who seem so admirably now to balance each other's strengths were not, I have to admit, chosen for that. They came, most of them, to an office across the street from the back door of the Yale School of Architecture, when I was chairman there and then Dean. As the ransacking of the office became routine, we longed for the country and found a place 35 miles from New Haven on the pleasant Main Street of Centerbrook, a middle class hamlet of Essex. But the move was not without its traumas: in 1971, shortly after I spent every penny I could lay my hands on buying a handsome old bit factory which backed up to a mill pond and dam, Richard Nixon suddenly put a moratorium on HUD projects, on which we were mostly working. HUD projects did not pay until final approval, so we were fully broke. It made a nice mess of ashes for Centerbrook to rise from. The firm could instead have aptly been called "Phoenix Architects."

Only some of the footsteps on the stairs belonged to the sheriff serving unpleasant papers. But we came to expect that every footfall was the knell of doom. We stopped refurbishing the premises and I borrowed vast sums from my brother-in-law to keep the sheriff and other wolves from the door. Then with everything temporarily under control in 1975, I heeded the call back to California. The successor firm to Charles Moore Associates—Moore Grover Harper—picked up the pieces with enthusiasm and things started looking up. There was, for instance, a large rainstorm that burst the dam, cleared a building site, and allowed us finally to construct most of the plans we had abandoned in 1971. So the place began to look complete.

But long before this, I had organized myself to sell the premises and the architects' office to what were then seven partners. We spent, I think, a year trying to figure out what to call ourselves so as to avoid sounding like a lawyers' office with seven names, and decided more descriptively on Centerbrook. We did continue to stress product over profit, and in fact managed to hold the profit at bay for years by throwing elaborate Halloween parties, the most amazing of which was probably the one with the 200-pound tap dancer.

What has evolved over the years (and I hope it works as well for the Confederation of Independent States) is a Federation of Independent Partners, who keep a subtle bond between them in what is for me a continuing astonishment. There is a weekly luncheon meeting, for instance (only one of which I have ever been to), where the competing requirements for help on many different projects is bargained for and ironed out with extraordinary efficiency and effectiveness—all between soup and nuts. The partners all help each other though their design signatures are now vividly different, and Jim Childress, as a new principal, will help launch Centerbrook into a new generation.

It's luck, but it's as though we had planned it.

Charles W. Moore
Austin, Texas

ABOVE: The first Board of Directors meeting, July 1976. Left to right: Jeff Riley, Glenn Arbonies, Charles Moore, Bob Harper, Bill Grover

LEFT: Principal Jim Childress surrounded by partners, from left, Bob Harper, Mark Simon, Bill Grover, Jeff Riley, and Chad Floyd.
Photo: Sarah Jenkins

$\mathcal{P}$ROJECT CREDITS

Riley House (pages 16-19)
Guilford, Connecticut, 1976 and 1986
Client: Jefferson B. and Barbara Riley
Project Designers: Jefferson B. and Barbara Riley
Awards: AIA House and Home Merit Award, 1977; Architectural Record House, 1978
Publications: House and Home, September 1977, Architecture d'Aujourd'hui, September 1977; Nikkei Architecture, 1978; Process Architecture #7, 1978; Solar Houses, Louis Gropp (pantheon Books, 1978); House & Garden, Spring 1978; Architectural Record, Mid-May, 1978; Affordable Houses Designed by Architects, Jeremy Robinson (Architectural Record Books, 1979); AIA Journal, Mid-May 1979; Perfect Home, April 1980; More Houses Architects Design for Themselves, Walter Wagner Jr. (McGraw-Hill, 1981); Process Architecture #21, 1981; Twenty Five Years of Record Houses, Herbert L. Smith Jr. (McGraw-Hill, 1981); New York Times, 1981; Award Winning Passive Solar House Designs, Jeffrey Cook (Garden Way, 1984); Metropolitan Home, May 1987; Remodeling, December 1990

Jones Laboratory (pages 20-21)
Cold Spring Harbor Laboratory
Cold Spring Harbor, New York, 1976
Client: Cold Spring Harbor Laboratory
Project Designers: William H. Grover and Charles Moore
Project Team: Ronald Eichorn
Consultants: John G. Nicholls (scientific advisor)
Contractor: Cold Spring Harbor Laboratory
Awards: Connecticut Society of Architects/AIA Award, 1980; AIA Honor Award, 1981
Publications: AIA Journal, Mid-May 1981; Architectural Record, April 1982; Houses for Science, Elizabeth Watson (Cold Spring Harbor Laboratory Press, 1991)

Waste Water Treatment Plant (pages 22-23)
Cold Spring Harbor Laboratory
Cold Spring Harbor, New York, 1976
Client: Cold Spring Harbor Laboratory
Project Designer: William H. Grover and Robert L. Harper, with Charles Moore
Landscape Design: James D. Watson
Contractor: Cold Spring Harbor Laboratory
Awards: Red Cedar Shingle Merit Award, 1981
Publications: Architectural Record, April 1982; Houses for Science, Elizabeth Watson (Cold Spring Harbor Laboratory Press, 1991)

Delbruck-Page Laboratory (pages 24-26)
Cold Spring Harbor Laboratory
Cold Spring Harbor, New York, 1981 & 1987
Client: Cold Spring Harbor Laboratory
Project Designer: William H. Grover
Project Team: John Salem (project manager, Delbruck); James R. Martin (project manager, Page)
Consulting Engineers: Besier Gibble Norden (structural); Energy Research Group (mechanical)
Contractor: Cold Spring Harbor Laboratory

Publications: Houses for Science, Elizabeth Watson (Cold Spring Harbor Laboratory Press, 1991)

Demerec Laboratory Addition (pages 26-27)
Cold Spring Harbor Laboratory
Cold Spring Harbor, New York, 1982
Client: Cold Spring Harbor Laboratory
Project Designer: William H. Grover
Project Team: James A. Coan (project manager)
Consulting Engineers: Besier Gibble Norden (structural); Energy Research Group (mechanical)
Publications: Houses for Science, Elizabeth Watson (Cold Spring Harbor Laboratory Press, 1991)

Grace Auditorium (pages 28-31)
Cold Spring Harbor Laboratory
Cold Spring Harbor, New York, 1986
Client: Cold Spring Harbor
Laboratory Designer: William H. Grover and James C. Childress, with Charles Moore (consulting)
Landscape Design Concept: Child Associates
Landscape Architect: Keith Simpson
Consulting Engineers: Besier Gibble Norden (structural); Energy Research Group (mechanical/electrical)
Consultants: Robert A. Hansen Associates (acoustics)
Contractor: A.D. Herman Construction Company
Awards: Connecticut Society of Architects/AIA Award, 1988; American Schools & Universities Citation, 1988; Long Island Chapter/AIA Award, 1988
Publications: Architectural Record, April 1982; Architecture, August 1988; American Schools & Universities, November 1988; Houses for Science, Elizabeth Watson (Cold Spring Harbor Laboratory Press, 1991)

Neuroscience Center (pages 32-37)
Cold Spring Harbor Laboratory
Cold Spring Harbor, New York, 1991
Client: Cold Spring Harbor Laboratory
Project Designer: William H. Grover and James C. Childress, with Charles Moore (consulting on conceptual design)
Project Team: Daniel Glynn, Jon Lavy, Susan Edler Wyeth, Kathleen Amrock, Michael Milne, Michael J. Crosbie, Sheryl Milardo, John D. Kennedy
Landscape Architect: Keith Simpson
Consulting Engineers: Besier Gibble Norden (structural); Energy Research Group (mechanical)
Contractor: A.D. Herman Construction Company
Publications: Houses for Science, Elizabeth Watson (Cold Spring Harbor Laboratory Press, 1991)

Rudolph House (pages 38-41)
Williamstown, Massachusetts, 1981
Client: Dorothy & Frederick Rudolph
Project Designers: Robert L. Harper and Charles Moore, with James C. Childress

Project Team: Frank Cheney
Landscape Architect**Landscape Architect:** Lester Collins
Consulting Engineers: Besier Gibble Quirin (structural); Energy Research Group (mechanical)
Contractor: Gordon Oakes
Awards: Builder's Choice, 1984
Publications: GA Houses 13; House Beautiful, January 1983; House Beautiful Building Manual, Fall-Winter 1984-85

Roanoke Design '79 (pages 42-43)
Roanoke, Virginia, 1979
Client: City of Roanoke, Virginia
Project Designers: Chad Floyd and Charles Moore
Project Team: Leonard J. Wyeth, Jefferson B. Riley, William H. Grover, Robert L. Harper, Dean Ruth, Glenn Arbonies
Associate Architect: Hayes, Seay, Mattern & Mattern
Landscape Architect: Lester Collins
Consulting Engineers: Hayes, Seay, Mattern & Mattern
Consultants: The American City Corporation (economics); Robert Morris (traffic); Brenda Huffman (graphic design); Freeman and Roberts (cost)
Awards: National Headliners Media Award, 1979; American Society of Landscape Architects Design Award, 1981
Publications: Urban Design International, July 1982; "Giving Form in Prime Time," The Scope of Social Architecture, C. Richard Hatch (Van Nostrand Reinhold, 1983); Architecture, November 1984.

Roanoke Markethouse (pages 44-45)
Roanoke, Virgina, 1985
Client: City of Roanoke, Virginia
Project Designer: Chad Floyd
Associate Architects: Timm Jameson of Hayes, Seay, Mattern & Mattern **Consulting Engineers:** Hayes, Seay, Mattern & Mattern
Consultants: Brenda Huffman Graphic Design (color)
Contractor: Fraun and Waldron
Publications: Architecture, October 1986

Simon-Bellamy House (pages 46-47)
Connecticut Shoreline, 1981
Client: Mark Simon and Penelope Bellamy
Project Designer: Mark Simon
Consulting Engineers: Besier Gibble Quirin (structural); Phil Fine, Energy Resource Group (solar)
Consultants: Mary Ann Rumney, Penelope Bellamy (color); Michael Haskins (interior design)
Contractor: Nelson Denny
Publications: House Beautiful, October 1981; New York Times Magazine, January 3, 1982; GA Houses 13, March 1983; AIA Journal, October 1983; Connecticut Magazine, March 1984; Newsday, April 29, 1984; Northeast Magazine, September 23, 1984; Boston Globe Magazine, March 5, 1989; Architectural Detailing in Residential Interiors, 1990

Rowe House (pages 48-51)
Connecticut, 1981
Project Designer: William H. Grover
Project Team: Stephen Lloyd, (project architect)
Landscape Architect: Lester Collins
Consulting Engineers: Besier Gibble Norden (structural)
Contractor: Post Road Wood Products
Publications: Architectural Digest, August 1983; The Atlantic, September 1984; Connecticut Magazine, February 1985; Builder, November 1986

Watkins Glen Master Plan (pages 52-53)
Watkins Glen, New York, 1980
Client: Schuyler County Industrial Development Agency
Project Designer: Chad Floyd and Charles Moore
Project Team: Mark Denton (project manager); Frank Cheney, Cindy Hamilton, F. Bradford Drake, James R. Martin, Jefferson B. Riley, Stephen Lloyd
Consulting Engineers: Cahn Engineers (transportation and cost)
Consultants: The American City Corporation (economics)
Awards: New York State Historic Conservation Award, 1985; AIA Certificate of Excellence in Urban Design, 1988; Excellence on the Waterfront Award, 1991
Publications: Architecture, May 1989

"Timespell" (pages 54-55)
Watkins Glen State Park
Watkins Glen, New York, 1982
Client: White River Development Corporation
Project Designer: Chad Floyd
Project Team: J. Whitney Huber (project manager)
Landscape Architect: Lester Collins
Consulting Engineers: Besier Gibble Norden (structural)
Consultants: Brenda Huffman Graphic Design; White Oak Design (sound and light show production)
Contractor: Dalrymple Contracting
Publications: Architecture, December 1986

Lenz Winery (pages 56-59)
Peconic, New York, 1982
Client: Peter and Patricia Lenz
Project Designer: Mark Simon
Project Team: Stephen Lloyd (project manager), J. Whitney Huber
Landscape Architect: Lester Collins
Consulting Engineers: Besier Gibble Norden (structural)
Contractor: James McGarry
Awards: Connecticut Society of Architects/AIA Design Award 1982; American Wood Council Award, 1983; Long Island Council/AIA Design Award, 1984.
Publications: New York Times Magazine, September 19, 1982; Architectural Record, April 1984; Progressive Architecture, June 1984; Beaux Arts III, 1985; Architekur und Wohnen, May 1985; Metropolitan Home, 1985; Emerging Voices, 1986

Elliott House (pages 60-63)
Ligonier, Pennsylvania, 1983
Client: Ann Elliott and Peter Gruen
Project Designer: Jefferson B. Riley
Project Team: Julia H. Minor
Consulting Engineers: Besier Gibble Norden (structural)
Awards: Connecticut Society of Architects/AIA Design Award, 1983; Architecture Record House, 1983
Publications: AIA Journal, Mid-May 1983; Architectural Record, Mid-May 1983; The New York Times Magazine, September 25, 1983; Casa Vogue, October 1983; Diversions, November 1984; Global Architecture Houses #15, 1984; World Residential Design (DNP America, 1989); Architectural Detailing in Residential Interiors, Wendy Staebler (Whitney Library of Design, 1989); The Home, Susan S. Szenasy (Van Nostrand Reinhold, 1989); American Architecture of the '80s, Donald Canty, Editor (AIA Press, 1990)

Cape Cod Cottage (pages 64-65)
Eastham, Massachusetts, 1984
Project Designer: Chad Floyd
Project Team: J. Whitney Huber (project manager)
Contractor: Geoffrey Willis
Awards: Renaissance/Remodeling Design Award, 1987
Publications: Remodeling, October 1986; Architecture, October 1987; Boston Globe Magazine, October 1988

Crowell Studio (pages 66-67)
Long Island, New York, 1984
Client: David and Joan Crowell
Project Designer: Mark Simon
Project Team: Leonard J. Wyeth (project manager)
Consulting Engineers: Besier Gibble Norden (structural)
Contractor: Clarke Smith
Awards: Long Island Council/AIA Gold Award, 1984; Architectural Record Houses Award, 1985; Builder's Choice Award, 1985; Cedar Shake and Shingle Bureau/AIA, 1985; New England Regional Council/AIA Design Award, 1986
Publications: New York Times Magazine, July 1, 1984; Architectural Record, Mid-April 1985; Beaux Arts III, 1985; Builder, October 1985; Metropolis, November 1986; Arte y Cemento, January 1987; GA Houses 21, February 1987; House Beautiful, July 1987

Campus Master Plan/Residence Hall "Suntraps" (page 68-69)
Quinnipiac College
Hamden, Connecticut, 1984
Client: Quinnipiac College
Project Designer: Jefferson B. Riley
Project Team: J. Whitney Huber and Leonard J. Wyeth (project managers)
Landscape Design: Centerbrook, with Lester Collins
Consulting Engineers: Besier Gibble Norden (structural)
Awards: Connecticut Society of Architects/AIA Public Space Award, 1988
Publications: American School & University, November 1985; Architecture, December 1985

Echlin Health Sciences Center (page 70)
Quinnipiac College
Hamden, Connecticut, 1989
Client: Quinnipiac College
Project Designer: Jefferson B. Riley
Project Team: Nick Deaver (project manager); John D. Kennedy, Michael A.P. Casolo, Matt Malakias, Sheryl Milardo
Consulting Engineers: Besier Gibble Norden (structural); J.E. Berning (mechanical); Russ Franzen (civil)
Consultants: Acentech (audio/visual); Brenda Huffman (graphic design)
Publications: American School & University, November 1990

Computer Center (page 71)
Quinnipiac College
Hamden, Connecticut, 1983
Client: Quinnipiac Collge
Project Designer: Jefferson B. Riley
Project Team: Leonard J. Wyeth (project manager); Charles Mueller, Sheri Lucero
Consulting Engineers: John L. Altieri (mechanical)

Dining Hall and Servery (pages 72-73)
Quinnipiac College
Hamden, Connecticut, 1988
Client: Quinnipiac College
Project Designer: Jefferson B. Riley
Project Team: Leonard J. Wyeth (project manager); Charles Mueller, Michael J. Crosbie, Sheryl Milardo
Consulting Engineers: Besier Gibble Norden (structural); John L. Altieri (mechanical)
Consultants: Crabtree McGrath (kitchen); Brenda Huffman (graphic design)
Awards: Renaissance/Remodeling Grand Award, 1990
Publications: Tile World, May/June 1990; Mangia, Summer 1990; Remodeling, January 1991

Carl Hansen Student Center (pages 74-75)
Quinnipiac College
Hamden, Connecticut, 1991
Client: Quinnipiac College
Project Designer: Jefferson B. Riley
Project Team: Leonard J. Wyeth (project manager, phase I); Ida Vorum (project manager, phase II); Jon Lavy, Robert Proctor, Daniel Glynn, Michael Milne, Michael J. Crosbie, Wan Wandrazi, Paul Shainberg, Sheryl Milardo, Margaret Wazuka
Landscape Design: Centerbrook, with Johnson & Richter
Consulting Engineers: Besier Gibble Norden (structural); J.E. Berning (mechanical); Russ Franzen (civil)

Residence Hall Village (pages 76-77)
Quinnipiac College
Hamden, Connecticut, 1991
Client: Quinnipiac College
Project Designer: Jefferson B. Riley
Project Team: Ida Vorum (project manager); Daniel Glynn,

Jonathan Parks, Michael J. Crosbie, Daniel Vickers, Michael Milne, David Altman, Wan Wandrazi, Robert Proctor, Sheryl Milardo, Margaret Wazuka
Landscape Design: Centerbrook, with Johnson & Richter
Consulting Engineers: Besier Gibble Norden (structural); J.E. Berning (mechanical); Russ Franzen (civil)

Private Library (pages 78-79)
New York, New York, 1985
Project Designer: Mark Simon
Project Team: Leonard J. Wyeth (project manager)
Consultants: Breakfast Woodworks (millwork)
Contractor: Gus Dudley
Awards: New England Regional Council/AIA Award, 1986; American Wood Council Award, 1986; Builder's Choice Award, 1987
Publications: New York Times Magazine, February 8, 1987; Remodeling, February/March 1987; Architecture, April 1987

Hood Museum of Art (pages 80-85)
Dartmouth College
Hanover, New Hampshire, 1985
Client: Dartmouth College
Project Designers: Charles Moore and Chad Floyd
Project Team: Glenn Arbonies (project manager); Richard L. King, James C. Childress, James A. Coan, James R. Martin, Stephen Lloyd, Leonard J. Wyeth, Julie Miner, Beth Rubenstein, Jenny Tate
Landscape Architect: Lester Collins
Consulting Engineers: Besier Gibble Norden (structural); Helinski Zimmerer (mechanical and electrical)
Consultants: Systems Design Associates (lighting and theater); Brenda Huffman Graphic Design; Ralph Ward (security); Freeman & Roberts (cost)
Awards: New England Regional Council/AIA Honor Award, 1986; AIA National Honor Award, 1987; Brick in Architecture Award, 1989
Publications: American Architecture of the '80s, Donald Canty, Editor (AIA Press, 1990); Architecture, January 1986; Architectural Record, February 1986; Abitare, September 1986

Baldwin House (pages 86-87)
Essex, Connecticut, 1985
Client: Dr. Robert Baldwin
Project Designer: William H. Grover
Project Team: Leonard J. Wyeth (project manager)
Landscape Architect: Lester Collins
Consulting Engineers: Besier Gibble Norden (structural)
Contractor: Keith Nolin
Awards: Builder's Choice Award, 1987
Publications: Metropolitan Home, December 1986; Architecture, July 1988, Better Homes & Gardens Building Ideas, Spring 1989

Samuel's Clothing Store (pages 88-89)
Roanoke, Virgina, 1985
Client: Samuel's Clothing Store
Project Designer: Chad Floyd

Project Team: James R. Martin (project manager); Sandy Scott
Consulting Engineers: Energy Research Group (mechanical)
Consultants: Systems Design Associates (lighting); Brenda Huffman Graphic Design
Publications: Architecture, January 1986

Andrews House (pages 90-93)
New Jersey, 1985
Client: Nancy & David Andrews
Project Designer: Robert L. Harper
Project Team: Leonard J. Wyeth, Jennifer Tate, Walker J. Burns, Beth Rubenstein
Landscape Design: David Andrews
Interior Design: Nancy Andrews
Consulting Engineers: Besier Gibble Norden (structural)
Publications: How to Plan and Design Additions (Ortho Books)

Student Center (pages 94-95)
Colby College
Waterville, Maine, 1986
Client: Colby College
Project Designer: Jefferson B. Riley
Project Team: J. Whitney Huber (project manager); Randy Wilmot, Jenny Tate, Sandra Vlock; Robert Coolidge, Roger Upham Williams, Glenn Arbonies, Elaine Larry, David Hajian, Charles Balfour
Consulting Engineers: Besier Gibble Norden (structural & civil); John L. Altieri (mechanical)
Consultants: Crabtree McGrath (kitchen)
Awards: American School & University Louis I. Kahn Citation, 1986
Publications: American School & University, 1986; Boston Globe, March 24, 1987; Architecture, May 1987; Food Service Magazine, 1988; Progressive Architecture, April 1990

East Hampton Library and Community Center (pages 96-99)
East Hampton, Connecticut, 1986
Client: Town of East Hampton, Connecticut
Project Designer: Mark Simon
Project Team: Stephen Lloyd (project manager)
Consulting Engineers: Besier Gibble Norden (structural); Energy Research Group (mechanical)
Consultants: M.A. Rumney Associates (graphics/signage)
Contractor: Naek Construction
Awards: Connecticut Society of Architects/AIA Design Award, 1988
Publications: Architecture, October 1988

Williams College Museum of Art (pages 100-105)
Williamstown, Massachusetts, 1986
Client: Trustees of Williams College
Project Designers: Robert L. Harper and Charles Moore
Project Team: Richard L. King, Dennis J. Dowd, Charles Mueller, Roger Upham Williams, Susan Edler Wyeth, David Hajian, Walker J. Burns, Robert Coolidge, Randy Wilmot
Landscape Architect: Lester Collins
Consulting Engineers: Spiegel & Zamecnik (structural, phase I); Flack & Kurtz (mechanical/electrical, phase I); Besier Gibble Quirin

(structural, phase II); Isidore Schiffman (mechanical/electrical, phase II)
Consultants: George Sexton (lighting, phase I); Joseph M. Chapman (security)
Contractor: Fontaine Brothers Construction Co. (phase I); Breadloaf Construction Co. (phase II)
Awards: Governors Design Award
Publications: ArtNews, January 1987; Architecture, February 1987; Interiors, September 1987

Reid House I (pages 106-109)
Cleveland Heights, Ohio, 1987
Client: Mr. & Mrs. James Reid
Project Designer: Jefferson B. Riley
Project Team: Walker J. Burns (project manager); Roger Upham Williams, Jean Smajstrala
Consulting Engineers: Besier Gibble Norden (structural); Energy Research Group (mechanical, electrical, plumbing)
Consultants: Susan Kent Kauer (landscape); Blodgett Hately Designs (interiors)
Awards: Builder's Choice Grand Award, 1988; Connecticut Society of Architects/AIA Design Award, 1988; Cedar Shake and Shingle Bureau Merit Award, 1989
Publications: Architecture, July 1988; Builder, October 1988; Builder, January 1989; House Beautiful, October 1989; Architectural Detailing in Residential Interiors, Wendy Staebler (Whitney Library of Design, 1989); House Beautiful Home Building, Fall/Winter 1990;

McKim House (pages 110-113)
Fisher's Island, New York, 1988
Client: Charlotte McKim
Project Designers: Mark Simon and Leonard J. Wyeth
Landscape Architect: Lester Collins
Awards: Cedar Shake and Shingle Bureau/AIA First Award, 1989; Connecticut Society of Architects/AIA Honor Award, 1989; American Wood Council Award, 1990; Builder's Choice Grand Award, 1990; New England Regional Council/AIA Design Award, 1990
Publications: House & Garden, June 1989; Design Times, July/August 1990; Builder, October 1990; Progressive Architecture, November 1990

Striar Jewish Community Center (pages 114-115)
Stoughton, Massachusetts, 1988
Client: South Area Jewish Community
Project Designer: Jefferson B. Riley
Project Team: Dennis Dowd (project manager); J. Whitney Huber, Susan Edler Wyeth, Mahdad Saniee, Robert Coolidge, Nick Deaver, Sheri Lucero, Matthew C. Conley; Sheryl Milardo
Consulting Engineers: Besier Gibble Norden (structural); John L. Altieri (mechanical); Shofield Brothers (civil)
Consultants: System Design Associates (lighting, theater); Acentech (acoustics)
Publications: Stone World, September 1989

Longmeadows House (pages 116-119)
Redding, Connecticut, 1989
Client: Walter Kukulka
Project Designer: Robert L. Harper

Project Team: William Riley, Sheri Lucero, Howard Rosenberg
Landscape Design: Walter Kukulka
Consulting Engineers: Besier Gibble Norden (structural)
Contractor: Walter Kukulka

Wriston Art Center (pages 120-125)
Lawrence University
Appleton, Wisconsin, 1989
Client: Lawrence University
Project Designer: Jefferson B. Riley
Project Team: Michael Hellinghausen (project manager); Walker J. Burns, David Hajian, Charles Mueller, James R. Martin, Jon Lavy, Jonathan Parks, Michael Milne, James A. Coan, Sheryl Milardo, Stacia Hazard
Landscape Design: Centerbrook, with Harold Ginke
Consulting Engineers: Besier Gibble Norden (structural); John L. Altieri (mechanical); Martenson & Eisele (civil)
Consultants: System Design Associates (lighting); Chapman Ducibella (security); Acentech (acoustics, audio-visual); Brenda Huffman (graphic design)
Awards: New England Regional Council/AIA Design Award, 1989; American School & University Citation, 1989; Fox Valley Excellence in Masonry Award of Merit, 1990
Publications: Exclusively Yours, October 1989; American School & University, November 1989; Architecture, January 1990

Ross-Lacy House (pages 126-129)
Sherman, Connecticut, 1989
Project Designer: Mark Simon and James C. Childress
Project Team: Charles Mueller (job captain)
Landscape Architect: Sylvia Surdoval
Contractor: Picton Construction Company
Awards: Builder's Choice Grand Award, 1990; New England Regional Council/AIA Design Award, 1990; Connecticut Society of Architects/AIA Design Award, 1990
Publications: New York Times Magazine, October 15, 1989; Architecture, March 1990; Builder, October 1990; Custom Builder, November 1990; Boston Globe, April 2, 1991; House Beautiful, June 1991

Harper House Porch (pages 130-131)
Centerbrook, Connecticut, 1989
Client: Robert & Patricia Harper
Project Designer: Robert L. Harper
Contractor: Triangle Building Associates

House on the Connecticut Shore (pages 132-135)
Connecticut, 1989
Project Designers: Chad Floyd and Susan Edler Wyeth
Project Team: Howard Langner, Steve Dadajian, Jonathan Parks, Matt Malakias
Landscape Architect: Lester Collins
Interior Design: Birch Coffey
Consulting Engineers: Besier Gibble Norden (structural); J.E. Berning & Associates (mechanical)

Consultants: Brenda Huffman Graphic Design (color)
Contractor: Baldwin & Baldwin
Awards: Red Cedar Shake and Shingle Honor Award, 1991; Builder's Choice Merit Award, 1991

East Lyme Library and Community Center (pages 136-137)
East Lyme, Connecticut, 1990
Client: Town of East Lyme, Connecticut
Project Designer: Mark Simon
Project Team: Leonard J. Wyeth (project manager), Jean Smajstrla (job captain)
Landscape Architect: Lester Collins
Consulting Engineers: Besier Gibble Norden (structural); J.E. Berning (mechanical/electrical)
Contractor: Aspinet Construction Company
Publications: Library Journal, 1990

Conklin House (pages 138-141)
New Jersey, 1990
Client: Dr. & Mrs. E. Foster Conklin
Project Designer: Robert L. Harper
Project Team: Susan Edler Wyeth, Sheryl A. Milardo, William Riley, Charles Mueller
Landscape Architect: Lester Collins
Consulting Engineers: Besier Gibble Quirin (structural); Rospond Associates (mechanical)
Contractor: Terpstra Construction Company

Pershing Point Plaza (pages 142-143)
Atlanta, Georgia, 1990
Client: Kingston Investors
Project Designer: Chad Floyd
Project Team: Dennis Dowd (project manager); Stephen Lloyd
Associate Architect: Rob Miller, Architect
Landscape Architect: Lester Collins
Consulting Engineers: Weems/Doar Engineers (structural); Newcomb & Boyd (mechanical and plumbing)
Consultants: Williamson & Associates (specifications); Brenda Huffman Graphic Design
Contractor: Nico
Awards: Connnecticut Society of Architects/AIA Honor Award, 1991

Augusciak House (pages 144-145)
Lyme, Connecticut, 1990
Client: Joseph & Maureen Augusciak
Project Designer: Robert L. Harper
Project Team: Howard Rosenberg, William Riley, Robert Protor, Carol Curren
Landscape Architect: Keith Simpson
Consulting Engineers: Besier Gibble Norden (structural)
Contractor: Post Road Wood Products, Inc.

House in Connecticut (pages 146-149)
Connecticut, 1990
Project Designer: Chad Floyd
Project Team: Roger Upham Williams (project manager); Sheri Lucero, James A. Coan, Rob Coolidge, Jonathan Parks, Matt Malakias, Michael A.P. Casolo
Landscape Architect: Lester Collins
Interior Designer: Parrish Hadley
Consulting Engineers: Besier Gibble Norden (structural); Energy Research Group (mechanical)
Contractor: W.R.T. Smith
Awards: Main House: Renaissance/Remodeling Design Award, 1990. Poolhouse: Renaissance/Remodeling Design Award, 1989; American Wood Council Design Award, 1989; Connecticut Society of Architects/AIA Honor Award, 1989; Builder's Choice Grand Award, 1990; New England Regional Council/AIA Honor Award, 1990.
Publications: Main House: Remodeling, January 1991. Poolhouse: Builder, October 1990

Woodlands Cabin (pages 150-151)
East Coast, 1991
Project Designers: Mark Simon with Mahdad Saniee and Evan Markiewicz
Project Team: Ann Patterson
Interior Decorator: Mariette Gomez Associates
Consulting Engineers: Spiegel Zamecnik & Shah (structural); J.E. Berning (mechanical)
Consultants: Donald Stettner and Robert Kren (craftsmen/builders)

Reid House II (pages 152-155)
Cape Cod, Massachusetts, 1991
Client: Mr. & Mrs James Reid
Project Designer: Jefferson B. Riley
Project Team: Jean Smajstrala (project manager); Kyra Hauser, Richard King, Michael J. Crosbie, Ann Patterson, Sheryl Milardo
Landscape Design: Centerbrook, with Bunker Stimson Solien Design **Consulting Engineers:** Besier Gibble Norden (structural); J.E. Berning (mechanical); William M. Warwick & Associates (civil)

Henderson Hall Computer Resources Center (pages 156-157)
Bard College
Annandale-on-Hudson, New York, 1991
Client: Bard College
Project Designer: Chad Floyd
Project Team: Jean Smajstrla (project manager); Steve Tiezzi
Consulting Engineers: Besier Gibble Norden (structural)
Consultants: Brenda Huffman Graphic Design
Contractor: Bard College Buildings & Grounds

Pond House (pages 158-161)
Martha's Vineyard, Massachusetts, 1992
Project Designers: Mark Simon and James C. Childress
Project Team: Paul Shainberg, Stephen Holmes, Kevin Henson, Leonard J. Wyeth, Sheryl Milardo, Jonathan Parks, Michael J. Crosbie, Robert Coolidge, Michael Milne, Richard King, Wan Maison Wanradzi, Paul Mellblom
Landscape Architect: Lester Collins
Consulting Engineers: Besier Gibble Norden (structural); Savage Engineering (mechanical)
Contractor: Doyle Construction

Mitchell-Haney House (pages 162-165)
Connecticut, 1991
Client: Susan Mitchell & Douglas Haney
Project Designer: Robert L. Harper
Project Team: Susan Edler Wyeth, Michael J. Crosbie, Tracy Davis, William Egan, Carol Curren
Consulting Engineers: Besier Gibble Norden (structural)
Contractor: Triangle Building Associates
Awards: Hartford Monthly Residential Design Award, 1991
Publications: Fine Homebuilding, April/May 1992

Killingworth House (pages 166-169)
Killingworth, Connecticut, 1992
Project Designers: William H. Grover and Nick Deaver
Project Team: MIcahel Garner
Consultants: Besier Gibble Norden (structural)
Contractor: A. J. Shea Constuction
Awards: Renaissance/*Remodeling* Best of the Year Award, 1992; New England Regional Council AIA Design Award, 1992; Connecticut Society of Architects/*Hartford Monthly* Residential Design Award, 1993

House in the Country (pages 170-173)
Connecticut, 1991
Project Designer: Chad Floyd
Project Team: Nick Deaver, Kevin Henson (project managers); Sheri Lucero
Landscape Architect: Lester Collins
Interior Designer: Dian Boone
Consulting Engineers: Besier Gibble Norden (structural); Klepper, Marshall & King (acoustic); J.E. Berning & Associates (mechanical)
Contractor: Bogaert Construction

Miller House (pages 174-177)
The Berkshires, 1991
Project Designer: William H. Grover
Project Team: Sheri Lucero (project manager), Walker J. Burns
Landscape Architect: Lester Collins
Interior Decorator: Connie Beale
Consulting Engineers: Besier Gibble Norden (structural)
Contractor: Lou Boxer

Marsh Estate (pages 178-183)
East Coast, 1991
Project Designers: Mark Simon with Mahdad Saniee
Project Team: William H. Grover, Sheri Lucero, Todd Delfosse, Jonathan Parks, Ann Patterson, Jean Smajstrla, Evan Markiewicz, Howard Langner, Rob Coolidge, Wan Wanradzi, Robert L. Harper, Glenn Arbonies, Kathleen Amrock, Chris Buckridge, Michael A.P. Casolo, James C. Childress, Matt Conley, Linda Couture, Carol Curren, Michael J. Crosbie, Dennis Dowd, Susan Edler Wyeth, William Egan, Daniel Glynn, Norman Gregory, Stacia Hazard, Kevin Henson, Vincent Jordon, John D. Kennedy, Nancy King, Richard King, Jon Lavy, Mimi Locher, Elizabeth MacAlpine, James R. Martin, Sheryl Milardo, Michael Milne, Leslie Pitcher, Rob Proctor, Howard Rosenberg, Paul Shainberg, Steven Tiezzi, Chris Todd, Mary Walsh, Margaret Wazuka, Randy Wilmont, Leonard J. Wyeth
Landscape Architect: Lester Collins, Oehme van Sweden
Interior Decorator: Mariette Gomez Associates
Consulting Engineers: Spiegel Zamecnik & Shah (structural); J.E. Berning (mechanical)
Consultants: Systems Design Associates (lighting)
Contractor: E.A. Baker
Awards: Connecticut Society of Archtects/AIA Unbuilt Projects Honor Award, 1990

AUTHOR AND CONTRIBUTORS NOTES

Michael J. Crosbie is an architect and a Senior Editor of *Progressive Architecture*, whose writings have also appeared in *Architecture* magazine, *The Hartford Courant, Domus, Fine Homebuilding, Historic Preservation*, and numerous other publications. He has taught architectural journalism as an adjunct professor at the Roger Williams University School of Architecture and has practiced with Centerbrook Architects. He lives with his family in Essex, Connecticut.

James D. Watson is most noted for his co-discovery with Francis Crick of the structure of DNA, for which he won a Nobel Prize in 1962. Since 1968 he has directed the Cold Spring Harbor Laboratory.

Charles W. Moore is a recipient of the American Institute of Architects' Gold Medal, whose architecture and writings on architecture have gained him international recognition.